OVERFLOWING PEACE

OVERFLOWING PEACE

What God Says About A Peace-Filled Life

TARA DEW

Brentwood, Tennessee

979-8-3845-2199-0

Published by B&H Publishing Group
Brentwood, Tennessee

Dewey Decimal Classification: 248.84
Subject Heading: PEACE / CHRISTIAN LIFE—
PEACE / BIBLE. O.T. PSALMS 23

Throughout this book, the author has added italics and bold for emphasis in Scripture.

Cover design by B&H Publishing Group. Illustrations by B&H Publishing Group and miniwide/shutterstock. Author photo by NOTBS staff.

1 2 3 4 5 6 • 29 28 27 26

To my Mom, Linda.

You were the first one to teach me to love
my Shepherd and His sheep.
I am forever grateful.

I love you,
Tara

Contents

Introduction

Overflowing Peace in a World That Is Peaceless

I can't tell you how much it means that you have chosen to read this book! After all, it is written on one of the most familiar and memorized passages in all the Bible. Maybe you grew up reciting this passage as a child in Sunday school. Or maybe you cling to these familiar words during difficult times. Though it is often read at funerals, I believe that Psalm 23, penned by King David centuries ago, contains words for every one of our lives today.

Friend, I wish I could be sharing these truths with you face-to-face over a cup of coffee. I would much rather be talking than writing anyway. But the privilege of serving you through the written word is not lost on me. I know this book will get into hands that I would not have the opportunity to serve in person. And I know that sometimes it's easier to pick up a book when you are on your lunch break, sitting in a carpool line, or from your bedside table before retiring for the night. I am thankful that I can serve you, wherever or whenever you read this book. Please know I have thought of you and prayed for you as I studied this familiar text. I believe these promises wholeheartedly, and have lived, breathed, experienced, and taught the lessons found in these pages.

And I'm so thankful to study these truths with you because I can imagine that you too may be struggling through the very same seasons I've faced. The seasons where you feel a total lack of peace. Where you are overwhelmed and running on empty. Where you feel like your life is a chaotic mess. My hope is that as you read these pages, you would feel like you have a friend sitting right beside you.

Sadly, peace is often lacking in our culture. Not only are our lives chaotic, but so is our nation and world. Wars rage. Politics devour. Racism divides. Peace is not the descriptor of our day. But God offers something remarkably different in His Word. He says that in Him, we can experience true peace.

I pray that God will meet you in His Word and teach you things that you didn't know before. I pray that after gleaning from the truths found in Psalm 23, you will love your Shepherd more than you do now and experience a life of peace in His care.

The Metaphor of Psalm 23

Through this book, we will explore a metaphor in which God explains His relationship to His people. This teaching technique is commonly used in the Bible because we typically understand difficult concepts more easily when they are compared to something we are already familiar with. God often uses the natural elements of our world to explain the supernatural aspects of our relationship to Him. In my first book, *Overflowing Joy*, we looked at Jesus's metaphor of the Vine and branches in John 15 to explain how His presence brings a life of complete joy. In this book, we will look at another metaphor: sheep with a shepherd. And it is my prayer that you will discover how your Shepherd's presence can bring a life of total peace for you, His sheep.

When David wrote this psalm, the shepherding lifestyle would have been second nature to the Israelites. After all, most of them were herders themselves or lived around shepherds. They were nomadic folk who spent their days surrounded by nature. But today, in the twenty-first century, we are far more removed from this agrarian way of life. Most of us live in towns or cities, where concrete is much more prevalent than green pastures, and water is found in running faucets rather than quiet brooks. But for us to truly understand God's lessons in Psalm 23, we need to understand this shepherding metaphor so that we don't miss the truths taught in God's Word.

Overview of This Book

Each chapter of this book will focus on a different image that David uses to teach us about our Shepherd and His care. We will look at the images of a shepherd and his sheep (chapter 1), pastures (chapter 2), water (chapter 3), paths (chapter 4), valleys (chapter 5), rods (chapter 6), staffs (chapter 7), feasts/tables (chapter 8), oil (chapter 9), and dwelling places (chapter 10). Since the Israelites would have naturally known much more about each of these things than you and I do, we must study them and seek to understand what God is teaching us through each one.[1] But as you will see, each image helps us to know a different attribute of who our God is and how we relate to Him.

One of the major objectives I have in this book is that I want you to see the connection between this psalm and Jesus Himself. I hope that you see, line by line, and image by image, that Jesus is the fulfillment of the Shepherd depicted in Psalm 23. Jesus is our Good Shepherd. He is the Provider of daily bread and living water. He restores our soul and is our Protector and Dwelling Place. In other words, while Psalm 23 certainly had a word for its original audience in its original time, it is ultimately a psalm about Jesus. And my prayer for you is that you will appreciate His sweetness toward us as we explore this psalm together.

Through the book, the main translation that I will be using is the Christian Standard Bible. However, I know this might not be the one you are most familiar with or maybe even the translation from which you memorized Psalm 23. But don't worry! I will add in the other translations because they add to the fullness of our understanding and comprehension. So, keep your eyes out for your favorite wordings of this familiar psalm.

In addition, before each chapter begins, you will see the entire chapter of Psalm 23 written out. I have bolded the verse that we will be looking at in the subsequent chapter, but I believe it is helpful to see it in the total context of the chapter. Though you might be tempted, please don't skip over that page. Read Psalm 23 in its entirety before you begin the next chapter, remembering what we have covered and looking ahead to what we will still discuss. I pray this exercise is an encouragement to you as you proceed through the book.

I will also be including many other Scriptures from both the Old and New Testaments so that you can see how these themes are not just isolated to Psalm 23. The promises and truths of Psalm 23 are woven in rich ways throughout the whole Bible. Your God is good, and His presence and compassion for His people can be seen from Genesis to Revelation.

Friend, our God invites you to have complete, total, and matchless peace that is only found in Him. So, let's dive in right from the beginning and take it word by word. David writes in Psalm 23:1, "The Lord is my shepherd, I have what I need." We have a good Shepherd. And in Him, we truly do have everything we need.

Resting in His peace,

Tara

The Lord is my shepherd;
I have what I need.

He lets me lie down in green pastures;
he leads me beside quiet waters.

He renews my life;
he leads me along the right paths
for his name's sake.

Even when I go through the darkest valley,
I fear no danger,
for you are with me;
your rod and your staff—they comfort me.

You prepare a table before me
in the presence of my enemies;
you anoint my head with oil;
my cup overflows.

Only goodness and faithful love will pursue me
all the days of my life,
and I will dwell in the house of the Lord
as long as I live.

Psalm 23

Chapter 1

Peace in the Shepherd: Our Good

Have you ever received a gift that you weren't expecting? At our wedding shower, we received many of the normal gifts from our wedding registry: everyday dishes, fine China, crystal, bedroom linens, towels, pots, pans, and kitchen appliances. But I can remember opening one gift that was not on our registry. It was a gift from my mentor, chosen just for us. As I opened the beautiful gold frame, I was taken aback by the hand-drawn sketch, set in a navy-blue mat. A lamb was nestled in a shepherd's bosom, and the shepherd was resting his face upon the sheep's head. It was, and still is, the most tender picture of a shepherd who loves his sheep. To this day—twenty-five years later—this piece of art is displayed on our living room bookshelf because I love it so much. And, friend, when I imagine the shepherd of Psalm 23, this beautiful sketch is what comes to my mind.

Our Shepherd Is the Lord Almighty

David begins Psalm 23 with "The LORD is my shepherd, I have what I need." What a truth-packed verse! It is the most essential statement in the whole psalm. If we truly believe this, then everything else will make sense. Therefore, this chapter will only focus on David's first five words: "The LORD is my shepherd." (Don't worry—we won't forget the second part of verse 1; it's in chapter 2.) It is important that we understand who God is before we look at what He does or how He acts.

Look at the name of God which David uses to start verse 1: "The LORD." In our English translations of Psalm 23, it is not written "Lord" with lowercase letters. God's name is written with all uppercase letters, "LORD." This means that David uses a special name that God gave to Himself. It is four Hebrew consonants, and the English transliteration is YHWH, pronounced "Yahweh." In our English Bibles, you will find it translated LORD, Yahweh, or Jehovah. Remember, names have meaning, especially in the Old Testament. We must understand the meaning of this name of God so that we can better interpret and understand who He is as our Shepherd.

Though God has more than 1,000 different names in the Bible, Yahweh is the name for God Almighty and stands alone as the most sacred. In Jewish tradition, Yahweh is too sacred to even utter aloud. Jewish priests could pronounce it only one time a year in the temple, behind the veil of the Holy of Holies. This name for God occurs more than 6,519 times in the Old Testament and is the name most closely linked to God's redemption of His chosen people.[2] It means the self-existing one who never had a beginning or has an end. The name Yahweh was first revealed to Moses at the burning bush in Exodus 3:13–15:

> Then Moses asked God, "If I go to the Israelites and say to them, 'The God of your ancestors has sent me to you,' and they ask me, 'What is his name?' what should I tell them?" God replied to Moses, "I AM WHO I AM. This is what you are to say to the Israelites: I AM has sent me to you." God also said to Moses, "Say this to the Israelites: *The Lord*, the God of your ancestors, the God of Abraham, the God of Isaac, and the God of Jacob, has sent me to you. *This is my name forever; this is how I am to be remembered in every generation.*"

Yahweh, the Great I AM, uses this name for Himself. And it is the name by which He has chosen to be remembered throughout all generations. While God uses "I AM" to communicate Himself as the self-existent, eternal God—the

One who was and is and is to come and has no beginning or end—He uses another name to communicate His covenant faithfulness to Israel especially. Though He needs nothing for His existence and is wholly self-sufficient and eternal, He reveals Himself as something even more to His chosen people: Yahweh. The LORD. This name reflects not just His creative power and self-sufficiency in a general way; on top of that, it reflects His faithful character to His own.

Said another way, "I AM" is who God is to the whole world, and Yahweh is a covenant-keeping God *with His people.* Notice the specific audience God has in mind when revealing this name: "Say this to the *Israelites.*" He made a covenant with Abraham, Isaac, and Jacob, and will keep His promises to their offspring for a thousand generations. "A thousand generations" is another way of saying over and over again, forevermore. And their offspring? Well, if you're in Christ, you're included in that (Gal. 3:29). Friend, because of these truths, you can trust that the Lord will do what He says He will do. He does not change. He is Yahweh to you—your all-powerful, self-sufficient, covenant-keeping God. And He always will be.

Here are a few other Scripture verses that use this name for God, displaying His unchanging, eternal, and almighty character, along with His faithfulness to His own:

> **Isaiah 42:8:** "I am the LORD. That is my name, and I will not give my glory to another or my praise to idols."

Psalm 83:18: "May they know that you alone—whose name is the LORD—are the Most High over the whole earth."

Jeremiah 16:21: "Therefore, I am about to inform them, and this time I will make them know my power and my might; then they will know that my name is the LORD."

Isaiah 41:4: "Who has performed and done this, calling the generations from the beginning? I am the LORD, the first and with the last—I am he."

Deuteronomy 7:9: "Know that the LORD your God is God, the faithful God who keeps his gracious covenant loyalty for a thousand generations with those who love him and keep his commands."

Friend, please do not miss this truth: Yahweh—the Great I AM—is eternal, self-sufficient, and almighty. And the same God, who created the world and redeemed the people from slavery in Egypt thousands of years ago, is the same covenant-keeping God of today. He is faithful, gracious, and loyal for a thousand generations. And this Lord is the one that David declares as the Shepherd: "Yahweh is my shepherd" (Ps. 23:1 Lexham English Bible).

We Are His Sheep

So if this covenant-keeping, almighty God is our Shepherd, do you know what that makes us? His sheep! Psalm 95:7 describes us this way: "For he is our God and we are the people of his pasture, the sheep under his care." Psalm 100:3 agrees: "Acknowledge that the LORD is God. He made us, and we are his—his people, the sheep of his pasture."

When we meditate on these verses, we realize that as the great I AM, our God made us, and as Yahweh, our God chose us out of the world and into His own fold. We are not just His creation in a general sense, though that is awe-inspiring itself. We are also His sheep—sheep He takes particular favor in and specific responsibility over.

And "sheep" is a really good description of us. Just like sheep, we can be foolish sometimes. We can get ourselves in some real messes. We need constant attention and care, because we are needy. We must have a shepherd who will provide and care for us.

In Ezekiel 34, God describes this need and how He stepped in to provide for His sheep as the Good Shepherd. The whole chapter describes this incredible provision, but I want to show you a few verses that are particularly poignant about God's personal involvement as our Shepherd. Notice all the "I" statements of God that include such promises for us as His sheep:

"'For this is what the Lord GOD says: See, I myself will search for my flock and look for them. As a shepherd looks for his sheep on the day he is among his scattered flock, so I will look for my flock. I will rescue them from all the places where they have been scattered on a day of clouds and total darkness. I will bring them out from the peoples, gather them from the countries, and bring them to their own soil. I will shepherd them on the mountains of Israel, in the ravines, and in all the inhabited places of the land. I will tend them in good pasture, and their grazing place will be on Israel's lofty mountains. There they will lie down in a good grazing place; they will feed in rich pasture on the mountains of Israel. I will tend my flock and let them lie down. This is the declaration of the Lord GOD. I will seek the lost, bring back the strays, bandage the injured, and strengthen the weak, but I will destroy the fat and the strong. I will shepherd them with justice. . . . Then they will know that I, the LORD their God, am with them, and that they, the house of Israel, are my people. This is the declaration of the Lord GOD. You are my flock, the human flock of my pasture, and I am your God. This

> is the declaration of the Lord God.'" (Ezek. 34:11–16, 30–31)

God Himself, the Great I AM, is our Shepherd. Ezekiel 34 says that He cares for us, His sheep. He searches for us, rescues us, guides us, feeds us, and lets us lie down in rich pastures. (Doesn't that sound a lot like Psalm 23?) He seeks those who are lost, restores the injured, and strengthens the weak ones. We are His flock and He is our Lord God.

When I was eight years old, I learned firsthand the important truth of having an attentive shepherd who did these things. My family lived in England for three months, while my dad worked overseas with his computer company, IBM. During our stint in the United Kingdom, my mom was fascinated by the many black-faced sheep grazing on the green hills south of London. So, for one of our field trips, she arranged a visit to a sheep farm for us. We walked around the farm with the shepherd as he told us about his daily routines. He showed us how he prepared their food. He called the sheep by name. He led them to the right pastures. He tended to their wounds. He fed the baby lambs with bottles to make sure they got enough nutrition. He knew their tendencies and behaviors. And he loved each one. He was a personal shepherd.

And that is who our God is to us. He is a Shepherd who knows His sheep. Jesus says in John 10:14, "I know my own, and my own know me." Friend, our Shepherd is the Lord, Yahweh who made heaven and earth. You can rest in His power and might. But you can also rest in the fact that we have a personal, intimate Shepherd who knows and loves His sheep. Listen to Isaiah 40:11: "He protects his flock like a shepherd; he gathers the lambs in his arms and carries them in the fold of his garment. He gently leads those that are nursing." He knows us, He loves us, and He carries us. He is our Shepherd, and we are His sheep.

Our Shepherd Is Personal

As I mentioned already, "The Lord" (or Yahweh) is the only name in Scripture used to describe the personal relationship that God has with His people. This is *His* particular, covenantal name for *Himself,* which declares how *He* desires to relate to *His* people. In the verses we explored above, it is clear God desires to call His chosen people by the name of "His" own sheep who are under "His" care and in "His" pasture (Pss. 95:7; 100:3). He is owning His side of things. Said another way, He looks at His people and considers them "*My* sheep." But what about the other side of the relationship? How far is the personal nature of God allowed to reach? Can His people dare to say "my" toward Him in return? This is exactly why David says, "The Lord is *my* shepherd" (Ps. 23:1). The intimacy goes both ways! David contrasts the greatness of Yahweh with the intimate, personal pronoun "my." In this one sentence, we see God's deity and transcendence contrasted with His humanity and eminence.

David juxtaposes the Almighty, powerful characteristics of God, with the tender, personal attributes of God. Yahweh is an intensely powerful yet personal God, who does not merely want to own His sheep in a one-sided way, but wants a relationship with His children.

Angel Martinez, one of the greatest American evangelists of the 1900s, understood this dynamic. He preached about this personal nature of God and the extent to which it reaches. He was saved in a Baptist mission in San Antonio, Texas, in 1935. Angel ended up preaching Christ for more than sixty years, witnessing some 500,000 accept Jesus as their Savior. He had the entire New Testament memorized and famously preached these words about God, his personal Shepherd:

> The Lord, who made the Universe, is *my* Shepherd.
>
> The same God, who made the stars, walks with me when my heart is broken in the valley of the shadow of death. The same God, who lit the sun and gave the stars their celestial push and placed them in their orbit, is *my* Shepherd.
>
> The same God, who took a carpet of green grass and put it upon the earth and nailed it down with beautiful flowers, is *my* Shepherd.

> The same God, who took the rainbow and wove it into a scarf and draped it about the shoulders of a dying storm, is *my* Shepherd.
>
> And the same God, who in the dawning of a new day opens the door of the morning and floods the world with light and beauty, is *my* Shepherd.
>
> The same God, who at evening time pulls down the shade of the nights and shoots it through the sunset fire, is *my* Shepherd.
>
> The Lord, the Lord, *my* Shepherd.[3]

My heart echoes these thoughts. Yes, indeed He is all of these things and more. He was Angel Martinez's shepherd. He was David's shepherd. But sister, He is your Shepherd too. Just as He looks upon you and says "My," you too get miraculous permission to return His gaze and say the same. Luke 12:7 says that He knows everything about you, even the hairs on your head: "Indeed, the hairs of your head are all counted. Don't be afraid; you are worth more than many sparrows." He knows your name. He knows the number of hairs on your head and those that have fallen out on the bathroom floor. He knows every nook, cranny, and wrinkle of your skin and of your heart. And He cares for you. I hope these words from Psalm 139:1–6 comfort you today:

> LORD, you have searched me and known me.
> You know when I sit down and when I stand
> up;
> you understand my thoughts from far away.
> You observe my travels and my rest;
> you are aware of all my ways.
> Before a word is on my tongue,
> you know all about it, LORD.
> You have encircled me;
> you have placed your hand on me.
> This wondrous knowledge is beyond me.
> It is lofty; I am unable to reach it.

You are fully known and fully loved by your God. He is a personal Shepherd.

Our Shepherd Is Good

Not only is our Shepherd almighty and personal, but He is also good. Just as David describes God as his Shepherd, Jesus describes Himself similarly in John 10 and adds a noteworthy adjective. Jesus says, "I am the *good* shepherd. The *good* shepherd lays down his life for the sheep" (John 10:11). And then just three verses later He repeats this truth again: "I am the *good* shepherd" (John 10:14). The word *good* is repeated three times in four verses. I think Jesus is trying to reiterate a truth to His listeners: He is *good*!

But what does it mean to be good? Jen Wilkin defines *good* this way in her book, *In His Image*:

> [God] is immutably good, unchangingly good. His goodness undergoes no increase or decline, nor does it waver. In him there is no darkness at all, nor has there ever been, nor will there ever be. He is good and he does good. There is no better version of him to come, no progress from good to better to best for him. God's goodness is his utter benevolence, the complete absence of malice. God does not, cannot, and need not improve with age. He is as good as he ever has been or will ever be. Perfectly good. Utterly good.[4]

God is totally good. There is nothing evil in Him at all. He does good and desires good for His children. He is benevolent and kind.

On Mt. Sinai, God proclaimed His name "Yahweh" to Moses and paired it with His attribute of goodness. Check out their interaction in Exodus 33:18–19: "Then Moses said, 'Please, let me see your glory.' He said, 'I will cause *all my goodness* to pass in front of you, and I will proclaim the name "the LORD" before you. I will be gracious to whom I will be gracious, and I will have compassion on whom I will have compassion.'"

So many Scriptures define God as good. One of my favorites is Nahum 1:7, which says, "The Lord is good, a stronghold in a day of distress; he cares for those who take refuge in him." But there are several other verses that declare His goodness and command our praise. Psalm 106:1 says, "Hallelujah! Give thanks to the Lord, for he is good; his faithful love endures forever." This phrase is repeated in three other psalms as well (Pss. 107:1; 118:1; 136:1)! God is good and worthy of our praise.

At New Orleans Baptist Theological Seminary, we partner with a ministry for men and women struggling with addictions. It is a 6-month live-in drug and alcohol rehab center called Bethel Colony. Through the program they learn about who God is by studying the Bible, as well as learning basic life skills, including a hard work ethic. I love these men and women, and celebrate the hard life changes they are making. I visit them often in the four businesses they operate in our neighborhood: a coffee shop, a thrift store, a snowball stand, and a car wash. One of the phrases that is displayed on their walls—and repeated often by these precious men and women—is: "God is good, all the time. And all the time, God is good." I find myself saying it often too. Yes, God is good.

Jesus is described not only as the good Shepherd throughout Scripture, but also as something more. Consider these passages, and see if you can spot what I mean:

> **John 10:11:** "I am the *good shepherd.* The *good shepherd* lays down his life for the sheep."
>
> **Hebrews 13:20:** "Now may the God of peace, who brought up from the dead our Lord Jesus—the *great Shepherd* of the sheep—through the blood of the everlasting covenant."
>
> **1 Peter 5:4:** "And when the *chief Shepherd* appears, you will receive the unfading crown of glory."

As I studied these three verses, I noticed something that we often glance over in these Scriptures. Did you see it too? Look again at the italicized adjectives above, right before the word *shepherd* in each verse. Jesus has inherent attributes as our Shepherd. He is described as good, great, and chief. He is supreme in His benevolence and care for His sheep. Let's unpack these verses and adjectives a little bit more together.

Jesus is good. John 10:11 defines Jesus as good because He "lays down his life for his sheep." To guard against a predator, a shepherd would lay down and sleep in the gate, or door, of the sheepfold. Since his sheep are his livelihood, he must protect them and be awakened at even the littlest hint of threat to his sheep. And Jesus chose to lay down and die for us, since sin and death are our greatest enemy. He was willing to pay the price for our sins with His own death. His goodness is displayed by His willingness to sacrifice Himself in death on our behalf.

Have you ever wondered why the Friday before Easter is called Good Friday? Our kids used to say, "There is nothing good about that day. Jesus died." Oh, but friend, His death shows His goodness. He laid down His life for you and for me. I love the modern hymn by Brook Hills Worship, called "At the Glorious Cross," which echoes these truths. Jesus hung on the cross, condemned for our sins. And what was the darkest day indeed became a good day. He gave up His life for us.[5]

Jesus truly is our Good Shepherd, because He willingly laid down His life, dying for us.

Jesus is great. Hebrews 13:20 defines Jesus as great because He was "brought up from the dead." As the famous pastor Adrian Rogers once said, "The Good Shepherd not only died for you—He lives for you!"[6] Christ's greatness is displayed by His resurrection.

The apostle Paul describes the importance of the resurrection of our Great Shepherd in 1 Corinthians 15:14–17 (NIV):

> And if Christ has not been raised, our preaching is useless and so is your faith. More than that, we are then found to be false witnesses about God, for we have testified about God that he raised Christ from the dead. But he did not raise him if in fact the dead are not raised. For if the dead are not raised, then

> Christ has not been raised either. And if Christ has not been raised, your faith is futile; you are still in your sins.

You see, it is a wonderful thing when a shepherd willingly dies for his sheep. He gave up his life for them. But what good does that do for the sheep? They are now left without protection, provision, and care. But praise the Lord, our Good Shepherd became the Great Shepherd because He was raised from the dead! Our sins are paid for, and we have a Risen King, who is alive. Your Shepherd lives forever and is able to guide us from His throne (Heb. 7:24–25). Jesus truly is our Great Shepherd, because He was brought up from the dead and is alive!

Jesus is chief. Lastly, 1 Peter 5:4 defines Jesus as our chief Shepherd because one day He will "appear," returning for His children. This sets Him above all other shepherds. His chiefness is described by His glorification and glorious return! No one knows when He will return for His sheep, but the Bible is clear that He will come back. I love the verses from 1 Thessalonians 4:14–18 that describe what that day will be like:

> For if we believe that Jesus died and rose again, in the same way, through Jesus, God will bring with him those who have fallen asleep. . . . For the Lord himself will descend

> from heaven with a shout, with the archangel's voice, and with the trumpet of God, and the dead in Christ will rise first. Then we who are still alive, who are left, will be caught up together with them in the clouds to meet the Lord in the air, and so we will always be with the Lord. Therefore encourage one another with these words.

It is encouraging to be assured that Christ will appear one day, isn't it? The longer we live in this broken world, and see the headlines on the news daily, the more we long for the day when He will come back and make all things right. Whether we experience our own resurrections, or meet Him in the clouds, it will be a glorious day! And I love that Jesus's return is the ultimate proof of His role as our Chief Shepherd!

Peace in Our Good Shepherd

My friend, as we consider the first part of the first verse of Psalm 23, may it create a sense of wonder in our hearts: "The Lord is my Shepherd." Yes, the Lord is the almighty Yahweh, the Creator of heaven and earth. But He is also your personal Shepherd, who created you and knows every hair on your head, thought of your mind, and longing of your heart. He is your Good Shepherd. He laid down His life for you and took away the penalty of your sin! Jesus is also your

Great Shepherd because He rose from the dead and dealt with the power of sin over life and death. Finally, He will come back for you one day, freeing you from the presence of sin forever! This makes Jesus your Chief Shepherd of all. He is victorious over sin and death, and that reality should allow your heart to be at peace.

Because of God's goodness, and because we get to know the risen "Lord" as "*my*" Shepherd, we can have a life of overflowing peace! We can live with such a genuine, spilling-over peace, despite what our circumstances look like. This is what the end of Psalm 23 describes in verses 5 and 6, "My cup overflows. Only goodness and faithful love will pursue me all the days of my life." We will talk about these verses more in later chapters, but it is important to connect the dots now. Because your Shepherd is so good, you can have a life of goodness, faithful love, and peace too! I love the hymn "He Lives" (also known as "I Serve a Risen Savior") and how it paints such a bright picture of our resurrection tomorrow and our hope for the struggles we have today. No matter what storms in this life you may have, we can rejoice because He is alive![7]

He desires for you to live a life of abundant peace because of who He is. Jesus is your Good Shepherd and He promises: "Peace I leave with you. My peace I give to you. I do not give to you as the world gives. Don't let your hearts be troubled or fearful" (John 14:27). Knowing He is your Shepherd—and you are His sheep—is just one way to experience a life of overflowing peace.

Questions to Consider

1. When you hear "The Twenty-Third Psalm," what memories come to your mind? When did you first hear or learn this psalm? Do you associate it more with funerals or the everyday aspects of your life?

2. How does knowing the meaning of "I AM" and "Lord" (Yahweh) bring you comfort and peace? How have you seen these attributes of God in your life?

3. Does knowing that you are *His* sheep and that Yahweh is *your* Shepherd (with His personal attributes) lead you to a life of overflowing peace? Why?

4. Fill in the blanks to make your own Angel Martinez's poetry line:

> The Lord, the same God who _________,
> is *my* Shepherd.

5. Which title for Jesus as your Shepherd impacted you the most: the Good Shepherd, the Great Shepherd, or the Chief Shepherd? Why?

6. Why can a life of overflowing peace come from the knowledge of Jesus's goodness as our Shepherd? In other words, how does His nature provide you with peace?

Verses for Reflection

ISAIAH 26:4

"Trust in the LORD forever, because in the LORD, the LORD himself, is an everlasting rock!"

REVELATION 1:8

"I am the Alpha and the Omega," says the Lord God, "the one who is, who was, and who is to come, the Almighty."

JOHN 10:27–28

"My sheep hear my voice, I know them, and they follow me. I give them eternal life, and they will never perish. No one will snatch them out of my hand."

JEREMIAH 12:3

As for you, LORD, you know me; you see me.

1 CORINTHIANS 8:3

But if anyone loves God, he is known by him.

PSALM 34:8

Taste and see that the LORD is good.
How happy is the person who takes
refuge in him!

PSALM 84:11

For the LORD God is a sun and shield.
The LORD grants favor and honor;
he does not withhold the good
from those who live with integrity.

The Lord is my shepherd;
I have what I need.

He lets me lie down in green pastures;
he leads me beside quiet waters.

He renews my life;
he leads me along the right paths
for his name's sake.

Even when I go through the darkest valley,
I fear no danger,
for you are with me;
your rod and your staff—they comfort me.

You prepare a table before me
in the presence of my enemies;
you anoint my head with oil;
my cup overflows.

Only goodness and faithful love will pursue me
all the days of my life,
and I will dwell in the house of the Lord
as long as I live.

Psalm 23

Chapter 2

Peace in the Green Pastures: Our Daily Bread

When our kids were little, we would fold their little hands before every meal. We taught them a simple prayer that has a catchy rhythm to it. Now my preschool-age nieces and nephews recite this common refrain before meals too. Maybe you are familiar with this child's prayer as well:

> *God is great, God is good,*
> *Let us thank Him for our food.*
> *By His hands we all are fed,*
> *Give us, Lord, our daily bread.*
> *Amen.*

I love the powerful truths tucked into this simple child's prayer. May it not be so familiar to us that we lose the awe and wonder in it! These five lines teach children that God is a great and good Father who provides for their daily needs. It heralds to children the same message that Psalm 23:1 encapsulates: "The LORD is my shepherd; I have what I need."

In chapter 1, we looked at God's nature in those first five words of Psalm 23: "The LORD is my Shepherd." Yahweh truly is great. And yes, He truly is good. He is Jehovah, the Great I AM. But He is also a personal and tender God who knows me, His sheep. He is *my* Shepherd. And He cares for me out of His goodness. Because of who my Shepherd is, I can have peace.

He Provides for My Needs

The end of verse 1 reminds us that, because we have God as our Shepherd, "I have what I need." At first glance, I thought there was a comma that joined these two statements in my Christian Standard Bible. But then, I looked more closely and realized it is a semicolon, which is a punctuation used to connect two independent but related clauses. The statement "I have everything I need" can stand on its own but is joined to the first statement "the LORD is my Shepherd" with a semicolon. This means the end of verse 1 is related to and flows directly from that first statement. I don't want to harp too much on the English punctuation, but I think this is an important decision that the translators made. They chose to put a semicolon here. It is as if they wanted us to know with confidence "I have what I need" precisely because God is my Shepherd.

I love *The Living Bible*, as it words verse 1 this exact way: "Because the Lord is my Shepherd, I have everything I need!" Other translations may be more familiar to you: "The LORD is my shepherd; I shall not want" (NKJV, ESV). This means that we are content and not desiring anything else. The NIV translation says it this way: "The LORD is my shepherd, I lack nothing." Every need, He has provided. Every longing, He has filled. *The Message* just seems to blurt out this realization: "GOD, my shepherd! I don't need a thing."

The truth that these different translations are conveying is this: We can say with confidence that we do not need anything because we have God as our Shepherd. Friend, we lack nothing and don't need a thing because of who He is. He provides for us generously and abundantly, meeting our every need, not because He happened to see us in trouble and felt a random pang of obligation—rather, because abundance and generosity and provision are at His core. Those things are who He is. He is the Lord, our Provider.

Another name for God that is used throughout Scripture is "Jehovah-Jireh." This name means "the LORD will provide" and was first used in Genesis 22, in the story of Abraham and Isaac on Mount Moriah. In a test of faith, God instructs Abraham: "Take your son, . . . your only son Isaac, whom you love, go to the land of Moriah, and offer him there as a burnt offering on one of the mountains I will tell you about" (Gen. 22:2). Scripture tells us that even though he didn't understand, Abraham was obedient by getting up early the next morning, saddling his donkey, splitting the wood, and setting out for the place God would tell him. He and Isaac, plus two servants, walked for three days with the looming knowledge of what was to come. But Abraham was a man of faith, trusting that "the boy and I will go over there to worship; then we'll come back to you" (v. 5). Abraham fully believed he would sacrifice his son and then God would just raise Isaac back up and they would return to the servants together. Hebrews 11:17, 19 tells us that, "By faith, Abraham . . . offered up Isaac. . . . He considered God to be able even to raise someone from the dead." Isaac, on the other hand, hasn't yet put the pieces together, and in his ignorance of what was coming, he asked a fair question. "The fire and the wood are here, but where is the lamb for the burnt offering?" (Gen. 22:7). Note the confident trust in his father's response, "God himself will provide the lamb" (v. 8).

Abraham was faithful to build the altar, arrange the wood, and then he bound his son Isaac, placing him on the altar on top of the wood. I'm sure this was not as simple and easy as the Scripture makes it out to be. Isaac is a strong teenage son. Even if he was told what was happening and chose to lay down willingly, can you imagine the heartache of Abraham as he sees his only son lying there on the pile of wood? And in the case Isaac did not go down without a fight, well, that would be a hard struggle between a young man and his elderly father.

Can you imagine the questions: "Why are you doing this to me? Why are you trying to kill me? Why would God ask you to do this? Don't you love me?" And yet, whichever way the scenario went, Abraham was still obedient, taking the knife "to slaughter his son" (v. 10).

But at this exact moment the angel of the Lord intervenes, "Abraham, Abraham!" (Anytime a name is mentioned twice in Scripture, you know God is about to change their life!) Just then, out of nowhere, a ram appears with its horns caught in the thicket. God had provided the lamb indeed! Abraham offered it as a burnt offering in place of his son. And then look at what he does next: "Abraham named that place The Lord Will Provide" (v. 14). Remember, friend: The Lord is our Provider. Jehovah-Jireh.

Here in New Orleans, we have a common saying: "Won't He do it?" Anytime something happens unexpectedly, but in line with God's character and promises, church folks will say this to one another. And I love it! Yes, won't He do it? Won't He respond to our needs? Won't He provide for us? One commentator said that "The Lord Will Provide" can also be translated "The Lord will see to it!"[8] In other words, God sees your needs and makes provisions for them. Philippians 4:19 promises, "And my God will supply *all your needs* according to his riches in glory in Christ Jesus."

Even though we commonly think that our greatest need is money, that is not true. Your greatest need is not even to have more clothes or a bigger house or more food. Paul

Chitwood, President of the International Mission Board, reminds Christians often that "the world's greatest problem can be communicated with one word—lostness."[9] Without Christ, people will die and be separated from God in hell forever. So more than food, more than clothes, more than money, we need Christ and the salvation He gives. Jesus provided this for us at the cross.

Similarly to Abraham giving up his only son, we are told in John 3:16 that God "gave his one and only Son, so that everyone who believes in him will not perish but have eternal life." Jesus is the perfect Lamb, God's provision for our sin. John the Baptist proclaimed this truth: "Look, the Lamb of God, who takes away the sin of the world!" (John 1:29). Jehovah-Jireh, the God who provides His only Son as "a lamb led to the slaughter" for you and for me is Jesus (Isa. 53:7; Acts 8:32).

Since our sins have been paid for on the cross by Jesus, we can honestly proclaim like David, "The Lord is my Shepherd; I have everything I need." We have a Shepherd who knows our needs and is attentive to them. Won't He see? Won't He act? Won't He do it?

Therefore, we can echo David's words: I lack nothing. I am not deficient. I have no needs. I am content and at peace, because He is my Lord, my Shepherd, my Provider.

He Provides Rest

In Psalm 23:2, the Psalmist declares: "He lets me lie down in green pastures." We will talk in the next section about those green pastures, and how they are vital for a sheep's nutrients and health. But let's not rush past those first five words: HE LETS ME LIE DOWN.

Sister, do you need permission to lie down for a few minutes? In our world today, so many people—but especially women—seem to derive their worth from their busyness. Our culture glorifies productivity and busyness! To rest seems counter-productive to our society because if you stop working, then you aren't getting ahead. But our souls require rest to survive! By being still, we are reminded that our value is not in what we do, but in whom we belong to. We are the beloved sheep of a Good Shepherd who lets us lie down.

Throughout Scripture, God places a command on His people to rest, first seen in Exodus 20:8–11. It is the fourth command in the Ten Commandments: "Remember the Sabbath Day, to keep it holy. You are to labor six days and do all your work, but the seventh day is a Sabbath to the LORD your God. You must not do any work—you, your son or daughter, your male or female servant, your livestock, or the resident alien who is within your city gates. For the LORD made the heavens and the earth, the sea, and everything in them in six days; then he rested on the seventh day. Therefore the LORD blessed the Sabbath day and declared it holy." Why do you think God commands His people to have a Sabbath rest? It is evident the Lord sees value in rest. He set an example of rest in Genesis and then commanded rest for His people in Exodus. Not only is this valuable for our body, soul, and spirit, but also in rest we are reminded that God alone is our Provider. It is our duty and privilege to find our rest in Him.

You are invited by the Lord to come and rest in Him. And that invitation does not stop in the Old Testament. In Matthew 11:28–29, Jesus says, "Come to me, all of you who are weary and burdened, and I will give you rest. Take my yoke upon you and learn from me, because I am lowly and humble in heart, and you will find rest for your souls." In Jesus, we can find our ultimate rest! He is the place where our striving for salvation ceases, which means he can be the place where all our other types of striving cease as well.

Not only does the Lord command and invite us to rest, but we are reminded in Psalm 23 that our Good Shepherd specifically wants His sheep to lie down to rest. Did you know that sheep will not lie down unless they have four basic needs met by their shepherd first? In Phillip Keller's book *A Shepherd Looks at Psalm 23*, four needs are described:

1. The sheep must be free from fears,
2. They must be free from friction with others in their herd,
3. They must be free from pests, and
4. They must be free from hunger.[10]

Let's take a closer look at each of these four needs of sheep and see how our Good Shepherd also meets these needs in our lives.

Free from fear. Sheep are generally helpless animals that cannot defend themselves. They are always the prey, with their short, weak legs and bad eyesight. They have no defense against the myriad of agile, fast, and strong predators that will chase them, like wolves, mountain lions, and coyotes. Sheep are vulnerable, lacking claws or fangs. They do not have the ability to escape danger by flying or climbing. Their only defense mechanism is to run. Therefore, if sheep are afraid of danger, they must remain standing, ready to run at any time. A sheep will not lie down willingly when they are afraid of being attacked.

In addition to being defenseless, they are timid, feeble creatures who get spooked easily. When one sheep gets scared or startled, the whole flock will run too, out of pure fear of the unknown. And predators are more likely to attack in the dark of night, when it is even harder for sheep to see. This is why we are told that "shepherds were staying out in the fields and keeping watch at night over their flock" (Luke 2:8). It is vital for a shepherd to be with his flock in the darkest night to protect them from potential predators. Only when a shepherd is nearby, will a sheep lie down and rest, knowing that they are protected and free from impending fears and dangers.

As a parent, I have even seen this truth with my children. When they were little and would have a nightmare, they would run into our bedroom and climb into our bed. As I held them, feeling their short, rapid breaths and wet tears, I would remind them that it was just a bad dream. Nightmares are not real. I would have them touch my face and feel my hugs and know that this was real, not the bad dream. One night, our youngest son, Samuel, after he calmed down, said, "Can I just sleep here? I feel safer when I'm with you." If you are a parent, I'm sure you have similar stories with your kids. Just our presence brings them comfort.

And that is the way it is with our Good Shepherd. There is nothing quite like the presence of my God to dispel fears or dangers in my life. Listen to the promise of 1 John 4:18: "There is no fear in love; instead, perfect love drives out fear." We will discuss this more in chapter 6, but for now I want to remind you that your Shepherd will protect you from the assaults of your enemies. Satan seeks to attack us when we are not looking, or when we're weak or in a dark season of life. There also might be human "wolves" that desire to harm us too. These come in the form of deceivers, unbelievers, or false teachers. But how wonderful it is to know that we have a Good Shepherd who sees these predators, warns us of them in His Word, and then equips us against their attacks. We can rest in His protection and love. The psalmist even recounted this truth in Psalm 4:8: "I will both lie down and sleep in peace, for you alone, Lord, make me live in safety." Our hearts and minds can be at peace, because He is with us. In His presence, we can rest. Because He is our Shepherd, we can lie down, free from fears.

Free from friction. Sheep are not only helpless against outside predators, but they are also defenseless against themselves. Another common calamity among sheep is unrest and rivalry in the flock. Because sheep are territorial and dominant, they will create friction within the group. They will butt heads to be the top sheep, and the worst offenders are often the oldest ewes. It is called a "butting order," because an older female sheep will boss the other sheep by headbutting them or driving them away from the green pastures or the bedding grounds. Other sheep maintain their position using the same butting tactics. To defend their order or protect their position, a sheep will not lie down and rest. Sometimes these jealous fights can even become bloody and deadly! This behavior causes irritability and restlessness and even weight loss among the flock—that is, until a shepherd intervenes. The shepherd's presence puts an end to all rivalry.

Just like a shepherd's presence dispels the friction among the sheep, Christ's presence dispels the jealousy or competition among us. He tears down the racial, socioeconomic, political, or personal walls between us. His presence brings us peace from friction. Listen to these beautiful words about Christ's work of reconciliation to free us from friction with others:

> For he is our peace, who made both groups one and tore down the dividing wall of

> hostility. In his flesh, he made of no effect the law consisting of commands and expressed in regulations, so that he might create in himself one new man from the two, resulting in peace. He did this so that he might reconcile both to God in one body through the cross by which he put the hostility to death. (Eph. 2:14–16)

Jesus is our peace. Friend, there should be no fighting at the foot of the cross! There should be no rivalry around the throne of God. Titus 3:1–2 commands us "to obey, to be ready for every good work, to slander no one, to avoid fighting, and to be kind, always showing gentleness to all people." And Paul says it even more bluntly in Romans 12:18, "If possible, as far as it depends on you, live at peace with everyone."

But you might be wondering *how* should we do this? First Peter 5:5–7 instructs us in the way to do this in the kingdom of God: "All of you clothe yourselves with humility toward one another, because God resists the proud but gives grace to the humble. Humble yourselves, therefore, under the mighty hand of God, so that he may exalt you at the proper time, casting all your cares on him, because he cares about you." Because your Shepherd cares for you and knows what you need, humble yourself and make "every effort to keep the unity of the Spirit through the bond of peace" (Eph. 4:3). Peace in your relationships will follow because humility is the key to unity. Stop fighting and head-butting your way in this world to be the top sheep, rising above someone else. Humble yourself and cast your cares on Him alone!

With Christ's presence and a posture of humility, I can rest. And friend, you can too. Because He is our Shepherd, we can lie down, free from friction with others.

Free from pests. Another common problem for sheep are pests. There are two kinds of insects that particularly cause trouble for sheep: flies and ticks. During the summer, these two insects will drive the sheep absolutely crazy! If infested, the sheep are tormented and unable to lie down and rest. Instead, they will run around frantically, stomp their legs, shake their heads, and run into trees to bring any relief from these pests!

Only a very diligent and attentive shepherd will treat his sheep to prevent pests from annoying their flock. A good shepherd dips his sheep in insect repellent to clear their fleece of ticks and to keep the flies from irritating and disturbing his flock. As soon as there is the slightest sign of disturbance from pests, a shepherd provides relief. When you see a quiet, content, peaceful flock, you know there is a good shepherd nearby.

And just like sheep, we need an attentive and aware Shepherd who cares for our disturbances too! I don't know about you, but sometimes my mind is plagued with pesty thoughts! Whether they come in the form of fears, worst-case scenarios, ever-expanding to-do lists, conversation replays, worries, or otherwise, it is hard to fall asleep with all the buzzing in my mind. But when I bring these to the Lord, His peace fills me just like Philippians 4:6–7 promises: "Don't worry about anything, but in everything, through prayer and petition with thanksgiving, present your requests to God. And the peace of God, which surpasses all understanding, will guard your hearts and minds in Christ Jesus." With His presence, I can rest. Because He is our Shepherd, we can lie down, free from pests.

Free from hunger. The last issue that plagues sheep is hunger. A sheep will not lie down and rest if its stomach is empty. A hungry sheep is ever on its feet, trying to find enough to eat to satisfy their hunger. I can relate to sheep on this one! I can't fall asleep with a growling, empty stomach either. Can you?

Now think about the words of Psalm 23:2: "He lets me lie down in green pastures." Most sheep around the world live in dry, semi-arid areas, where it is not natural or common to find green pastures. If you've ever been to Israel, you know what I mean! It is a dry, brown, rocky desert. That means green pastures don't just happen. If sheep were to have green pastures to lie down in—free from hunger among the rocky terrain—the shepherd had to provide it! A shepherd must spend days clearing out roots, stumps, and rocks. Then, he must plow the field and plant the grass, irrigating it with water until it reaps a pasture that feeds their flock! A well-fed sheep in a green pasture is a sign of a providing shepherd.

Jesus knows that food is one of our most basic needs, and His Word tells us that He will provide it for us. Consider these promises found in Matthew 6:25–27, 31–34:

> "Therefore I tell you: Don't worry about your life, what you will eat or what you will drink; or about your body, what you will wear. Isn't life more than food and the body more than clothing? Consider the birds of the sky: They don't sow or reap or gather into barns, yet your heavenly Father feeds them. Aren't you worth more than they? Can any of you add one moment to his life span by worrying? . . . So don't worry, saying, 'What will we eat?' or 'What will we drink?' or 'What will we wear?' For the Gentiles eagerly seek all these things, and your heavenly Father knows that you need them. But seek first the kingdom of God and his righteousness, and all these things will be provided for you. Therefore don't worry about tomorrow, because tomorrow will worry about itself. Each day has enough trouble of its own."

Satisfying our hunger is just one example of the many ways the Lord meets our needs. As this passage makes clear, our basic needs include not just food, but water, clothing, shelter, and so on. This passage helps us realize that while our

Good Shepherd is most concerned about our spiritual needs, He is also concerned about our physical needs. They are not too small for Him. He knows what it takes for humans to survive on this earth, and He has created the earth in order to support that survival. He knows when the pantry runs low. He sees when the roof leaks. He is paying attention when the kids outgrow their clothes and there's not quite enough left in the bank account this month to get them brand-new ones. I have story after story in my own life, telling the glories of the Good Shepherd who saw these types of situations and provided for me out of nowhere. I'm sure you have those stories too. And it's all because He is our Shepherd, who sees our cares and helps us lie down, free from hunger.

But, friend, I hope that as we've been discussing these four fears, you can also see this important truth: For a sheep to be free from fears, frictions, pests, and hunger, they must depend on the Shepherd! Sheep cannot fix any of these on their own. They can't defend themselves from dangerous predators, they can't settle the rivalries between the sheep, they can't rid themselves of the flies or ticks, and they can't plow their own green pastures. "It is actually [the shepherd alone] who makes it possible for them to lie down, to rest, to relax, to be content and quiet and flourishing."[11]

Just like sheep, we have a Good Shepherd who provides rest for us. He is Jehovah-Jireh, our Provider. *The Message* paraphrases Psalm 23:2 this way: "You have bedded me down in lush meadows." Jesus's presence can free us from fears, frictions, pests, and hunger. He alone meets our needs and lets us lie down in green pastures.

He Provides Daily Bread

We just covered the idea of our Good Shepherd meeting the need of our hunger. Before we move on from this idea of God providing our food in green pastures, let's spend some time considering a specific *kind* of food the Bible often speaks of (along with how Jesus fulfills its deeper meaning). Just as a shepherd provides a green pasture for his sheep, Jesus provides daily bread for us.

This daily bread was first shown when the Israelites were wandering in the wilderness. They didn't have food and were complaining of hunger, so God told Moses, "I am going to rain bread from heaven for you" (Exod. 16:4). Can you imagine raining bread? Bread is perhaps my favorite food group, so this sounds like pure heaven to me! This manna that God sent down from heaven were flakes that were sweet like honey. And every morning, the Israelites were instructed to collect the manna to satisfy their hunger for that day. If they collected more than what they needed, it would spoil with worms. Deuteronomy 2:7 reminded the Israelites: "The LORD your God has been with you these past forty years, and you have lacked nothing." Doesn't that remind you of Psalm 23:1? "The LORD is my shepherd, I lack nothing" (NIV).

Likewise, on two occasions, Jesus feeds thousands of people in the countryside of Galilee. These miracles reenact the miracles in Moses's day when God provided manna from heaven. In John 6:30–35 a crowd returns to Jesus, hoping for more food. Instead, Jesus makes a radical "I am" statement in response to their requests:

> "What sign, then, are you going to do so we may see and believe you?" they asked. "What are you going to perform? Our ancestors ate the manna in the wilderness, just as it is written: 'He gave them bread from heaven to eat.'"
>
> Jesus said to them, "Truly I tell you, Moses didn't give you the bread from heaven, but my Father gives you the true bread from heaven. For the bread of God is the one who comes down from heaven and gives life to the world."
>
> Then they said, "Sir, give us this bread always."
>
> "I am the bread of life," Jesus told them. "No one who comes to me will ever be hungry."

Thinking back to the manna in the wilderness, Jesus reminds this crowd that God provided the bread for His people. Instead of performing a miracle for them, Jesus calls

Himself "the bread of life" (John 6:35). He doesn't just want to meet their physical needs, but their deeper spiritual needs also. This is the first of the seven great "I AM" statements of Jesus in the book of John.[12] But this one is interesting because Jesus is saying "I AM your manna that has come down from heaven."

Just as the sheep need good, green grass every day, bread for these first-century humans was vital to their survival. They couldn't just go to their local grocery store and pick up a loaf of bread in a variety of flavors. Bread was essential to their diet, and Jesus is describing Himself as essential to their daily spiritual life. Jesus is life to them!

But there is a deeper layer to Jesus being our "Bread of Life." Yes, He is to be our daily bread, meeting both physical and spiritual needs. But we need to remember that without bread, there is no life. And when Jesus says, "I am the Bread of Life," it is another way of saying: "Without My death, you cannot live."[13] He modeled this at the Last Supper with His disciples, the night before He was crucified: "And he took bread, gave thanks, broke it, gave it to them, and said, 'This is my body, which is given for you. Do this in remembrance of me'" (Luke 22:19). Jesus's death on the cross—His body, our bread, broken—made a way for us to live and never be hungry again. Just as the Israelites in the desert had to trust God daily for their manna, we must put our full trust in Him, who provides the only way of salvation. Doesn't this change how you read the Lord's Prayer in Matthew 6:9–13?

> "Our Father in heaven,
> your name be honored as holy.
> Your kingdom come.
> Your will be done
> on earth as it is in heaven.
> Give us today our *daily bread.*
> And forgive us our debts,
> As we also have forgiven our debtors.
> And do not bring us into temptation,
> But deliver us from the evil one."

Jesus truly is our manna, our daily bread, our bread of life. He *is* all we need.

Peace in Our Shepherd's Provision

My friend, as we consider these first two verses of the 23rd Psalm, may it bring a sense of peace to your heart: "The LORD is my shepherd; I have what I need. He lets me lie down in green pastures." God is your Shepherd and He will provide for you. He imparts freedom from fears and dangers. His presence provides deliverance from pests and hunger. And in His provision—both for our ordinary needs and our eternal needs—we can have a life of overflowing peace.

We can honestly say with the psalmist, "I lack nothing!" Because He is my Shepherd, I can lie down and rest in His provision. He alone gives me peace. Peace from predators and dangers. Peace from pests and disturbances. Peace from a gnawing hunger. I love this line from a famous hymn: "Savior, like a shepherd lead us; much we need Thy tender care; In Thy pleasant pastures feed us, For our use Thy folds prepare: Blessed Jesus, Blessed Jesus, Thou has bought us, Thine we are."[14]

Most importantly Jesus has given us peace with God through His death. He gives us salvation as God has provided the Lamb. He is Jehovah-Jireh, the God who provides. Colossians 1:20 reminds us that we are reconciled to God as Jesus was "making peace through his blood, shed on the cross." Jesus's death is the provision for our peace. And by trusting that He is our bread of life, we can experience a life of overflowing peace.

Questions to Consider

1. On a scale of 1 to 10, how content do you feel in life right now (with 1 = not at all and 10 = most content)? Why? What do you feel like you are lacking?

2. How have you seen God provide for you, as your Jehovah-Jireh?

3. Do you agree with Dr. Chitwood that the greatest need in the world today is not poverty or crime, but is lostness? Why or why not?

4. What keeps you from resting? What keeps you up at night? Do you have fears, friction with others, pests, or hunger?

5. How does knowing that Jesus is our living bread, whose body was broken for us, comfort you and bring you peace?

Verses for Reflection

JAMES 1:17

> Every good and perfect gift is from above, coming down from the Father of lights, who does not change like shifting shadows.

PROVERBS 3:24

> When you lie down, you will not be
> afraid;
> you will lie down, and your sleep will
> be pleasant.

PSALM 136:25

> He gives food to every creature.
> His faithful love endures forever.

MATTHEW 14:16–21

Jesus told them. "You give them something to eat."

"But we only have five loaves and two fish here," they said to him.

"Bring them here to me," he said. Then he commanded the crowds to sit down on the grass. He took the five loaves and the two fish, and looking up to heaven, he blessed them. He broke the loaves and gave them to the disciples, and the disciples gave them to the crowds. Everyone ate and was satisfied. They picked up twelve baskets full of leftover pieces. Now those who ate were about five thousand men, besides women and children.

JOHN 14:27

"Peace I leave with you. My peace I give to you. I do not give to you as the world gives. Don't let your heart be troubled or fearful."

The LORD is my shepherd;
I have what I need.

He lets me lie down in green pastures;
he leads me beside quiet waters.

He renews my life;
he leads me along the right paths
for his name's sake.

Even when I go through the darkest valley,
I fear no danger,
for you are with me;
your rod and your staff—they comfort me.

You prepare a table before me
in the presence of my enemies;
you anoint my head with oil;
my cup overflows.

Only goodness and faithful love will pursue me
all the days of my life,
and I will dwell in the house of the LORD
as long as I live.

Psalm 23

Chapter 3

Peace in the Quiet Waters: Our Living Water

Close your eyes and imagine the most peaceful place on earth to you. What did you envision? Did you picture the ocean, with the waves lapping along the beach? Did you picture a waterfall, flowing down from a rocky cliff? Did you imagine a little brook bubbling over smooth river rocks? Did you picture the sunset over a lake that is so still it mirrors the trees around it?

For most people, the peaceful place they envision includes some type of lake, river, or sea. Did yours? For me and my family, the most serene places always include water. For several years, we owned a camper and would slip away once a month as a family, adventuring to a secluded campground to escape the hustle and bustle of the city. We loved sitting around the campfire or hearing the crickets and cicadas at night. We loved drinking our coffee or hot chocolate in the camping chairs as the birds would sing all around us and squirrels would find their next snack. But most of all, we loved the water views. We would always try to find a campsite that overlooked the bay, a lake, a river, or even a creek. There is just something so calming about being around water. We could sit for hours and just watch the ripples expand, currents splash down a ravine, or waves come in and out with the tide. Somehow being in nature and around water relieves stress and brings a calmness and ease that wasn't there before.

The Need for Peaceful Water

I was astounded when I recently discovered that almost three-fourths of the world's surface is covered in water! Between the sky and the water, the majority of our planet is blue, which scientists have said is the most calming color due to its longer wavelength and relaxing properties. When you are around an ocean, a lake, or a river, not only does the color relax you through the use of your vision, but other effects of water also ground you through the use of all your other senses. Think about when you are sitting on the beach, staring at the ocean waves breaking on the shore. You hear their repetitive, constant sound. You smell the warm beach air. You feel the cool water lapping at your feet and the wet sand under your toes. You sometimes even can taste the saltiness of that ocean. You look out over that great expanse where 96.5 percent of the world's water resides. You stare at the distant horizon, where the ocean meets the sky, and you exhale.

Whenever we are around water, we sense a feeling of relaxation. Scientists have called it the "rest and digestive state," where the parasympathetic nervous system lowers our heart rate and blood pressure while increasing digestion and relaxation overall.[15] Throughout history the ancient civilizations found water to be essential and relaxing. Both the Greeks and the Romans built their empires around water, even figuring out how to bring water into their main city centers through aqueducts and other clay piping. They built spas with pools in their ancient gymnasiums, encouraging the citizens to partake in the relaxation that water brings.

Water is such a beautiful reminder of our Almighty God who created it all. He is our faithful God "who enclosed the sea behind doors when it burst from the womb, . . . [and] determined its boundaries . . . [declaring], 'You may come this far, but no farther; your proud waves stop here'" (Job 38:8–11). God reminds us that when we stare at the ocean, it should increase our respect for Him alone: "Do you not tremble before me, the one who set the sand as the boundary of the sea, an enduring barrier that it cannot cross? The waves surge, but they cannot prevail. They roar but cannot pass over it" (Jer. 5:22). The Lord God is the Creator of heaven and earth, and He is the commander of all the waters therein. The peace we are able to find near water is a gift from the Lord and a testament to His great power.

The Need for Drinkable Water

Of all the resources on planet Earth, water is the most important. We can survive for one month without food, but if we lack water for only one week, we perish. This is why in the popular book series *The Hunger Games*, Katniss Everdeen is reminded that her priority is to find water. When the survival games began, she didn't need to find food. She didn't need to find weapons. She didn't even need to form an alliance. All she had to do was find a source of clean water. Her trainer, Haymitch, warned her: "When you're in the middle of the games and you're starving or freezing, some water can mean the difference between life and death."[16] He knew that without water, she would die.

A human's body is made up of 60 percent water,[17] and a sheep's body is composed of about 70 percent water.[18] Drinking clean water leads to bodies that are strong, healthy, and full of vitality. But like humans, one of the major health challenges for sheep is dehydration. If sheep don't have access to enough water, they will become sick, sluggish, and weak. Dehydration can lead to many other issues in a flock. On average, a sheep needs two to four gallons of water every day.[19]

Sheep primarily receive their water from three main sources: (1) a well, (2) dew on the grass, or (3) streams. We will talk about the "quiet streams" in the next section, but let's consider the first two sources right now. A good shepherd—especially one who is raising sheep in an arid, desert context—will know where to find a well to water his sheep. These wells would often be placed along the common paths between grazing pastures and accessible to shepherds for their flocks. But if a shepherd has a green pasture, like we talked about in the last chapter, a well isn't necessary. The early morning dew on the green grass will provide all of the water that a sheep needs, as they are foraging for their food. God provides a sheep's daily intake of water with just the little drops of dew that form on the green pastures overnight.

In Judaism, dew symbolizes God's heavenly blessing, provision, prosperity, and renewal.[20] But its absence was associated with divine punishment.[21] In Numbers 11:9, we are told that it accompanied the manna that God rained down from heaven for the Israelites in the wilderness. How beautiful that each day, God provided food and water for His people. But centuries later, when they disobeyed, Elijah warned King Ahab, "As the Lord God of Israel lives, in whose presence I stand, there will be no dew or rain during these years except by my command!" (1 Kings 17:1). The presence or absence of dew was a reminder to the people of God's blessing or curse. God even promises them that if they repent, "I will be like the dew to Israel" (Hosea 14:5). And His Word and promises should "settle like dew, like gentle rain on new grass and showers on tender plants" (Deut. 32:2). Isn't that a beautiful picture of God's presence and promises to His people? (This word study has been particularly fun because it is also my last name!)

Before the sun rises, sheep will graze and forage on the green grass filled with dew. And then, as the day begins and the sun dries up the dew, sheep lie down and rest, full of both provision in food but also nourishment in water. All their needs have been provided for. They aren't hungry or thirsty. And they lie down in the green pastures, chewing their cud, in the "rest and digestive" state mentioned above. Knowing this about green pastures and the dew of the fields helps us understand even more what David was trying to communicate when he followed "I have what I need" with "He lets me lie down in green pastures." Green pastures are not just comfy places to take a nap, friend. For a sheep, and for us, they make a life-and-death difference.

The Need for a Shepherd to Lead Us to Still Waters

As wonderful as green pastures are, however, there are times they might not be available to a grazing flock. In Psalm 23:2, David continues with an alternative: "He leads me beside quiet waters." In the absence of an acceptable pasture, sheep need to be led to water that they can drink. One of the most important things a shepherd does is lead his sheep to clean, safe water. Without water, they will perish. They need a shepherd who will lead them.

Did you know that 80 percent of illnesses around the world today are because of unsafe water? Physical diseases and illnesses come from drinking unclean and unsanitary water from unsafe sources. Today, 703 million people (which is 1 in 11 people worldwide) lack access to clean water. And more than 1,000 children (under the age of 5) die each day from diseases related to lack of clean water or sanitation.[22] Listen to this shocking statistic: "Children under five are on average more than 20 times more likely to die from illnesses linked to unsafe water and bad sanitation than from conflict. . . . The reality is that there are more children who die from lack of access to safe water than by bullets."[23]

Just like these young people who have been harmed by unclean water, sheep have also been known to drink polluted water—water that is dirty and full of algae or parasites. When these things are consumed, it can cause diarrhea and other gastrointestinal issues. It can also cause the sheep's stomach to fill with gases, resulting in discomfort and sometimes death. If a shepherd can't quickly rid a sheep of gas, parasites, or diseases it will become cast—a term that references when a sheep has turned itself on its back, legs straight up in the air, and cannot get up. In other words, the sheep will find itself flipping over and dying. Clean drinking water is as important for a sheep's health and vitality as it is for humans.

Not only does the shepherd need to lead his sheep to water that is clean, but he must also find water that is safe for the sheep. My husband, Jamie, calls this "Goldilocks water."

It can't be too fast. It can't be too stagnant. It must be just right. So not only does a shepherd need to lead his sheep to clean water, it also has to be "quiet" (Psalm 23:2 in CSB and NIV). But other translations will say "still waters" (ESV, NKJV). *The Message* paraphrases it this way: "You find me quiet pools to drink from." No matter if the Hebrew word is translated as "quiet" or "still," it means the shepherd must lead his sheep to water that is moving but not rushing. If the water is going too fast, the clumsy, top-heavy, wool-laden sheep will be swept away in the loud rushing waters. Like chapter 2 mentioned, sheep are timid. They cannot swim very well and fear the noise and danger of fast-moving water. However, if the water is too stagnant, then the chances of algae and parasites grow exponentially creating poor-quality drinking water. A shepherd must lead his sheep to not just water, but "quiet waters."

And I love that throughout the Bible, our God is described as a Shepherd who will lead us to the waters that bring life. Sweet water. Clean water. Safe water. Quiet water. Waters of life, not death. Our God knows what we need and provides it for us. The Lord is so kind and aware of exactly the nourishment we need, but also the pace at which we can "lap up" His living water without running the other direction in fear. Look at these promises found in Isaiah 49:8–10:

> This is what the LORD says: "I will answer you in a time of favor, and I will help you in the day of salvation. I will keep you. . . .

> They will feed along the pathways, and their pastures will be on all the barren heights. They will not hunger or thirst, the scorching heat or sun will not strike them; for their compassionate one will guide them, and lead them to springs."

Don't miss that truth tucked into the last statement: Our God is the compassionate One! It is from His never-ending, sacrificial love and compassion that He guides us and leads us to the waters of life.

Jeremiah 31:9 echoes this truth too: "I will lead them to wadis filled with water." A wadi is normally a dry valley or riverbed in the desert, only filling with water when it rains. But we see in Scripture where our God does what He says He will do. He is a covenant-keeping God! First Kings 17:2–6 describes a time of drought under King Ahab's rule. But God led His servant, Elijah, to this wadi filled with water:

> Then the word of the LORD came to him: "Leave here, turn eastward, and hide at the Wadi Cherith where it enters the Jordan. You are to drink from the wadi. I have commanded the ravens to provide for you there."
>
> So he proceeded to do what the LORD commanded. Elijah left and lived at the Wadi Cherith where it enters the Jordan. The ravens kept bringing him bread and meat

> in the morning and in the evening, and he would drink from the wadi."

Our Shepherd not only is Jehovah-Jireh who makes provisions for our need for bread, but also leads us to sources of water for our hydration. Jesus is described in Revelation 7:17 in this same way: "For the Lamb who is at the center of the throne will shepherd them; he will guide them to springs of the waters of life, and God will wipe away every tear from their eyes." Just like sheep, we need a shepherd who will lead us to quiet waters. And the Bible promises that we indeed have One. Our Shepherd's name is Jesus!

The Need for Jesus to Give Us Living Water

Not only do we have a Shepherd who will guide us to the quiet waters, but we have a Shepherd who describes Himself as the giver of divine Living Water! I love this scene recorded in John 4. Jesus is traveling north from Judea to Galilee, and the Bible says that he "had to travel through Samaria" (v. 4). Now, because they hated the Samaritans and considered them half-breeds and heretics, any good Jew avoided Samaria like the plague! But Jesus *had* to go to Samaria, because He was about to change a woman's life forever. This precious woman was at a well, drawing water in the middle of the day. Normally women would go together to the well either early in the morning or later in the evening, when it was cooler and easier to do this daily task with others. But when Jesus arrives in Samaria, He finds a woman by herself at the well. This scene itself tells us that she was lonely, outcast, and without friends, going to the well when no one else was there. We later find out that she had five husbands and was currently living with someone who was not her husband. Ostracized by her society, either by her own poor choices or unfortunate circumstances against her, it is no wonder she was at the well by herself.

Jesus defies all cultural norms and expectations when He talks to this Samaritan woman and asks her for a drink (John 4:7). A good Jewish rabbi would never talk to a Samaritan, let alone a Samaritan woman. To share a drinking cup with her would be scandalous and unclean! This is why she responds to His request with a question, "'How is it that you, a Jew, ask for a drink from me, a Samaritan woman?' . . . For Jews do not associate with Samaritans" (v. 9). But I love Jesus's reply in verses 10 and 14, "If you knew the gift of God, and who is saying to you, 'Give me a drink,' you would ask him, and he would give you living water. . . . Whoever drinks from the water that I will give him will never get thirsty again. In fact, the water I will give him will become a well of water springing up in him for eternal life." Jesus is promising her that He is the One with the authority and kindness to give not only Himself, but also the living water of the Holy Spirit to all those who believe in Him. Jesus explains a few chapters later, "'If anyone is thirsty, let him come to me and drink. The one who believes in me, as the Scripture has said, will have streams of living water flow from deep within him.' He said this about the Spirit" (John 7:37–39). You see, when we receive Jesus for who He says He is, we will be filled with the springs of Living Water inside us—the Spirit of Life!

After saying this to the Samaritan woman, Jesus patiently answers her questions, talks theology with her, and then reveals that He is the Messiah (John 4:26). It was this news that changed her life forever! She leaves one of her most valued possessions—her water jar—and runs into town to tell them about Jesus (v. 28)! She is one of the first evangelists. The very people that she was ostracized from, the women she wouldn't go to the well with, are now the very people that she tells the good news of Jesus to! And note the importance of what she says, "Come, see a man who told me everything I ever did! Could this be the Messiah?" (v. 29). The Bible says that many believed in Jesus because of her testimony (v. 39). She had found the giver of true Living Water and couldn't wait to tell others about Him. In Jesus, she found fulfillment like she had never found in husbands or relationships, and she would never be thirsty again.

Have you ever accepted Jesus to be your Messiah? To be your Savior and fill you up with the ever-bubbling Living Water of His Spirit? I was five years old when I met Him. I was at a Billy Graham crusade with my mom and grandparents. And even though I had grown up in a Christian home, I heard the gospel that night in a way that changed my life forever. Dr. Graham explained that I was a sinner and could never be good enough to enter heaven. My good works would always fall short of the standard of a holy God. But God loved me so much that He sent His Son, Jesus, to die on the cross for my sins, and through His death, I could have eternal life. That night, I walked down front with my fifty-five-year-old Grandma and we both accepted Jesus. No longer was I trying to satisfy my thirst with good words or perfectionism! I met the giver of Living Water that night, and He filled me up!

My husband's testimony is very different than mine. Jamie did not grow up in a Christian home. Instead, his home was broken by divorce when he was only seven years old. His life began to spiral downward as he couldn't read, failed two grades, and was put in special needs classes. He tried to find his value, identity, and satisfaction in different things, like band, sports, and even friends. But nothing quenched his thirst. By the eighth grade, he was into drugs and alcohol, and by his junior year in high school, he had been arrested twice. He moved about three and a half hours away to live with his dad, and through the invitation of Christians at his high school, he went to a Centrifuge summer youth camp in Panama City Beach, Florida. During the worship service on the first night, he gave his life to Christ. After years of drinking from diseased and parasitic things of this world, he was filled by the Living Water! And now, the boy who failed two grades in elementary school because he couldn't read has two doctoral degrees and has authored eight books. He is a Philosophy professor and the President of New Orleans Baptist Theological Seminary. Jesus changes lives!

I see so many people in our world today who are seeking to quench their thirst with all the wrong things. Our culture is plagued by addictions to alcohol, drugs, and other substances. Others try to find their thirst quenched by material possessions, job titles, or money. Still, others are drinking from social movements or religious cults that leave them more confused and depressed. Jeremiah 2:13 warns: "For my people have committed a double evil: They have abandoned me, the fountain of living water, and dug cisterns for themselves—cracked cisterns that cannot hold water." Instead of finding peace and satisfaction in Jesus, so many have trusted in empty wells that just leave them thirstier.

Jesus invites us to come to Him and drink of His Living Water! He says in Revelation 21:6–7: "I am the Alpha and the Omega, the beginning and the end. I will freely give to the thirsty from the spring of the water of life. The one who conquers will inherit these things, and I will be his God, and he will be my son." He freely gives the Spirit, the water of life! He desires for you to be His child, and generously gives us His salvation with mercy, grace, and peace that we do not deserve. With His arms stretched wide, it is our job to just reach out and accept the gift. Drink deeply from Him. Pray that you would thirst for Him, like Psalm 42:1–2 describes: "As a deer longs for flowing streams of water, so I long for you, God. I thirst for God, the living God." He offers us His Living Water, and we need Him.

Peace in His Living Water

When my oldest daughter Natalie was a little girl, she was swinging on our playset one afternoon. With this contemplative look in her eye, she said, "I wish this world was full of rainbows and butterflies and unicorns and sparkles. Oh, if only the world had peace." I don't know what prompted that idealist comment, but it made me smile. All I could reply was, "Me too, honey."

This world is longing for peace. Isn't that the stereotypical answer for every beauty pageant contestant? "I just want world peace." But it's true. At the heart of every addiction, every longing, every struggle is the desire for peace. Peace from fighting with others. Peace from internal conflict. Peace from the struggles and strife. This is why we long for serene places, both in God's creation and internally too.

And we find it in Jesus! His peace is quiet, still, and nourishing to our souls, like living water. This reminds me of Psalm 1:1–3 that equates a blessed life to "a tree planted beside flowing streams, that bears its fruit in its season, and its leaf does not wither. Whatever he does prospers" (v. 3). Just like the sheep beside the quiet waters, the person who is like this tree beside the flowing streams does not participate in evil. She delights in the Lord's instruction and meditates on it day and night. She is one that follows the Shepherd's leading to waters of life, walking by the Spirit of Christ who lives inside her.

Our peace is not found in this world or in our circumstances, possessions, or life. Our peace is found in our Shepherd, who leads us beside quiet waters, and is Himself the giver of Living Water—the Spirit of Life who sustains us when we would otherwise perish! In Jesus alone, we can have a life of overflowing peace.

Questions to Consider

1. What peaceful place did you envision when this chapter began? Did it include water? Why is water so peaceful to you?

2. Have you ever "thirsted" for the wrong things? Drunk from unsafe or unclean water, which just leaves you sicker? What sinful things (empty cisterns) have you tried to find your satisfaction in?

3. Do you have a testimony of when you met Jesus, your Living Water? If not, do you want to meet Jesus today? Please see the appendix of how to accept Christ.

4. Maybe your story is like the woman at the well. Or maybe you have a story like mine or Jamie's. But either way, God has given you a story. Who do you need to share it with? Who might believe because of your story?

5. Why is water the most important resource for life? How does Jesus, as our Living Water, meet this vital need in our spiritual lives?

Verses for Reflection

EZEKIEL 34:14–15

> "I will tend them in good pasture, and their grazing place will be on Israel's lofty mountains. There they will lie down in a good grazing place; they will feed in rich pasture on the mountains of Israel. I will tend my flock and let them lie down. This is the declaration of the Lord God."

JEREMIAH 31:25

> "For I satisfy the thirsty person and feed all those who are weak."

ISAIAH 8:6–8

"Because these people rejected the slowly flowing water of Shiloah . . . the Lord will certainly bring against them the mighty rushing water of the Euphrates River—it will overflow its channels and spill over its banks. It will pour into Judah, flood over it, and sweep through, reaching up to the neck."

MATTHEW 5:6

"Blessed are those who hunger and thirst for righteousness, for they will be filled."

REVELATION 22:17

Both the Spirit and the bride say, "Come!" Let anyone who hears, say "Come!" Let the one who is thirsty come. Let the one who desires take the water of life freely.

ISAIAH 58:11

"The Lord will always lead you, satisfy you in a parched land, and strengthen your bones. You will be like a watered garden and like a spring whose water never runs dry."

The LORD is my shepherd;
I have what I need.

He lets me lie down in green pastures;
he leads me beside quiet waters.

He renews my life;
he leads me along the right paths
for his name's sake.

Even when I go through the darkest valley,
I fear no danger,
for you are with me;
your rod and your staff—they comfort me.

You prepare a table before me
in the presence of my enemies;
you anoint my head with oil;
my cup overflows.

Only goodness and faithful love will pursue me
all the days of my life,
and I will dwell in the house of the LORD
as long as I live.

Psalm 23

Chapter 4

Peace in the Right Paths: Our Renewing Righteousness

Our family has been laughing so hard this week because we have watched and rewatched a video that was circulating across the internet. It is absolutely hilarious and shows just how dumb and undiscerning sheep are!

The video starts with a close-up shot of a shepherd pulling on the leg of a sheep that is wedged head-first into a small ditch. The sheep is bleating loudly for help. The shepherd yanks and yanks on its hind leg until finally he frees the sheep from this rut. The sheep, in total excitement, begins to bound away. But in a few short leaps, it bounds right back into the ditch. The shepherd throws his hands up and then goes to free the sheep again.

Stories like this are such a true depiction of us. We can get ourselves into some ditches! And we are totally stuck and helpless until by God's grace, He frees us from our rut. Then, we are free and leaping along, and before we know it we land right back in the same trouble again! I'm reminded of Isaiah 53:6, "We all went astray like sheep; we all have turned to our own way." We surely get ourselves into trouble, time and time again.

Like Sheep, We Need to Be Renewed

Just like that foolish sheep in the video, I need a shepherd. This is why David continues in Psalm 23:3, "He renews my life." Other translations say, "He refreshes my soul" (NIV) or "He restores my soul" (ESV and NKJV). Not only do the green pastures and the still waters renew and refresh us physically, but also our Shepherd Himself brings a restoration that we so desperately need! In later chapters, we will talk about the tools a Shepherd uses to restore us (His rod, staff, and oil), but for now, I want us to just pause and think about how the shepherd's very presence can refresh and renew his sheep.

Left to their own devices, a sheep can get stuck in terrible positions. Not only can sheep find themselves in precarious ditches, but they also are easily *cast*—a term, as we learned in the last chapter, that references when a sheep has turned itself on its back, legs straight up in the air, and cannot get up. We talked about this with the rushing waters, but sheep can even become cast on uneven surfaces. Flailing and frustrated, the sheep has no ability to right itself. If left in this cast position, a sheep will die within a few hours. The gases in a sheep's stomach rise and cause them to suffocate and have a heart attack. Without a shepherd's attentive care, a cast sheep is a dead sheep. However, a good shepherd, who notices a sheep in this position, will come to their rescue. Rolling them to their side, a shepherd corrects a sheep's digestive and respiratory tracts allowing them to breathe correctly. Maybe this is why *The Message* paraphrases Psalm 23:3 as "You let me catch my breath." But then standing the sheep upright, a shepherd will straddle it between his legs and let the circulation be restored to its lower extremities. Then, he will rub the sheep's legs to restore feeling and movement as the blood returns. After a few moments, the sheep can take some wobbly steps and be renewed along the right path.

In addition to rushing waters or uneven ground, overgrown, matted, dirty wool can also cause a sheep to become cast. If sheep are not cared for, their fleece can become so long and thick that they become rather top-heavy. They are then more likely to lose their balance and fall over, flipping right onto their back. To renew and restore his sheep's balance and ability to walk steadily, a shepherd needs to shear them. By removing the heavy, dirty, matted wool, it lightens the sheep's load and allows them to walk more easily. *The Living Bible* phrases Psalm 23:3 in a way that really resonates with this thought: "He gives me new strength." With a smaller fleece and lightened load, a sheep indeed has new strength to walk. His strength has been renewed.

Like sheep, we can become downcast. Maybe you feel like the terrain of life has been too uneven and unstable to get any good footing, leaving you helpless and flailing. Maybe you feel like your load is too heavy to bear. Maybe you are anxious and worried, unable to see how you can right yourself in this position. Or maybe, friend, you feel like you are suffocating and can't breathe. David puts into words what so many often feel: "Why are you cast down, O my soul? And why are you disquieted within me?" (Ps. 42:11 NKJV)

But take heart! We have a great Shepherd who renews us! My friend, your God loves you so much that He doesn't just leave us in our helpless state. He doesn't ignore our pleas. He doesn't see our predicament and turn aside unwilling to help. I love this promise found in Psalm 121:1–3: "I lift my eyes toward the mountains. Where will my help come from? My help comes from the LORD, the Maker of heaven and earth. He will not allow your foot to slip." Our God will come to us, find us, and set our feet back on solid ground! Look how Psalm 103:4–5 describes the restoration of our God: "He redeems your life from the Pit; he crowns you with faithful love and compassion. He satisfies you with good things; your youth is renewed like the eagle." Our Good Shepherd truly renews and restores us!

However, we must do our part in turning to Him and accepting His help! A sheep who resists the shearing of the Shepherd will only continue to add more burden to the load. Sometimes, we love our ways more than His ways. Sometimes, we love our sin more than our Savior. And just like a sheep needs shearing, we need to cast off our sins on the Lord so they don't weigh us down, letting Him remove them from us. Listen to the command found in Hebrews 12:1–2: "Therefore, since we also have such a large cloud of witnesses surrounding us, let us lay aside every hindrance and the sin that so easily ensnares us. Let us run with endurance the race that lies before us, keeping our eyes on Jesus, the pioneer and perfecter of our faith." Just like sheep need to be rid of their matted, heavy fleece, we need to willingly throw off every sin and obstacle in order to walk rightly too! We must accept the restoration of our Savior.

Like Sheep, We Prefer Familiar Paths

In addition to their clumsiness and likelihood of becoming cast, sheep also have a propensity toward familiarity. They like to travel along the same rutted paths and go to the same pastures. Familiarity brings comfort to them. They are creatures of habit. Same trail. Same tracks. Same furrows. Same fields.

The problem with this is that a well-worn path has grooves and crevices caused by constant traffic. On paths like this, a sheep can get its foot stuck in one of these ruts. These ditches can cause a twisted ankle or hurt hoof quickly.

In addition, well-worn paths lead to pastures that are overgrazed by the sheep. These wastelands have no green grass left. Everything that is edible has been eaten! And the brown grass that is left behind is polluted with manure. Diseases and parasites abound. Yet a sheep will choose the familiar path and pasture any day, even if it is not for their good. On top of this, a well-worn pathway also makes for easy hunting by predators.

Oh, my friend, how often I act the same way! I want things that are familiar. I want what is comfortable. I want what I have known and experienced before. I can be so very stubborn and stiff-necked, thinking that my way is the best way. Proverbs 14:12 echoes this truth: "There is a way that seems right to a person, but its end is the way to death." Just like a sheep choosing the familiar path that leads to the over-grazed, polluted places, we might choose the comfortable and well-known paths too, but they will lead to our destruction.

You see, friend, when we get comfortable with the familiar, we have no need for endurance or self-discipline in looking for the better things. We become lazy and self-indulgent, satisfied only on the "what is" and not "what could be." And we don't want to trust our Shepherd to lead us to new places. Just like sheep, we like our familiar paths.

Like Sheep, We Need a Shepherd to Lead Us on New Paths

An American shepherd described sheep this way: "There is no other class of livestock that requires more careful handling."[24] A good shepherd won't let his sheep move along their same familiar trenches or graze in their wasteland pastures. He must lead his sheep down new paths. A shepherd must have a plan for rotating his flock through pastures and grazing fields, which means the sheep must be kept on the move. He must lead and guide them on new paths to new pastures.

This is why David declares that God "leads me along the right paths for his name's sake" (Ps. 23:3). These paths might be new to us, but they are known by the Shepherd—and they are *right.* That is why some translations say, "He leads me in paths of righteousness" (ESV and NKJV) or "you . . . send me in the right direction" (MSG). God will not allow us to stay on our same old, familiar, rutted paths. He leads us to new paths, for our righteousness and good. I love the promises found in Jeremiah 29:11, "'For I know the plans I have for you'—this is the LORD's declaration—'plans for your well-being, not for disaster, to give you a future and a hope.'" Our Good Shepherd has a plan for our good. He knows the right paths. We must trust Him.

There are so many examples in Scripture of God leading His people, but perhaps the greatest story is found in Exodus. The Israelites had been enslaved for more than 400 years and were being oppressed more and more. Finally, after God's warnings to Egypt's king and the ten plagues that followed, the people were released from their bondage. Moses led this free nation out of Egypt and into the wilderness on the way to the Promised Land. But something interesting happened: God led His people on a different route. Not the one they would have expected. Not the familiar path and certainly not the comfortable one. Look at these verses in Exodus:

> When Pharaoh let the people go, God did not lead them along the road to the land of the Philistines, even though it was nearby; for God said, "The people will change their minds and return to Egypt if they face war." So he led the people around toward the Red Sea along the road of the wilderness. . . . The LORD went ahead of them in a pillar of cloud to lead them on their way during the day and in a pillar of fire to give them light at night, so that they could travel day or night. The pillar of cloud by day and the pillar of fire by night never left its place in front of the people. (Exod. 13:17–18, 21–22)

The way didn't make sense to the people, but in God's wisdom, He guided them on a new path that was for their good. And more significantly: He never left them. He guided them with a cloud during the day and a pillar of fire by night. He is a Good Shepherd, who led the people of Israel on a new path that was best. Just two chapters later, the people sing a new worship song to the Lord for what He has done: "LORD, who is like you among the gods? Who is like you, glorious in holiness, revered with praises, performing wonders? . . . With your faithful love, you will lead the people you have redeemed; you will guide them to your holy dwelling with your strength" (Exod. 15:11, 13). Yes, who is like our God? Who else leads and guides His people on just the right path with faithful love and strength?

In my life, there have been many times when I have preferred my familiar, comfortable ways. After all, for more than thirty years, I lived in the same town. I knew all the roads. I knew all the shortcuts. I knew all the stores. I knew the churches and the people. I had my friends, my family, my home. Life was comfortable and familiar. But God wanted to lead our family down a new path about six years ago, when my husband became the president of New Orleans Baptist Theological Seminary. We loved our familiar paths back in our home state of North Carolina, but as we followed God to Louisiana, we learned about His leading in a whole new way. And this path was for our good! Our family is thriving in New Orleans, and we love our city of music, art, food, and culture. Not to mention, we now get to lead thousands of men and women as they prepare for ministry.

Another time when God led me on a new path was three years ago when the opportunity came to write my first book, *Overflowing Joy*! I never dreamed I would be a writer or author. I loved teaching and speaking! So this new path of communicating through the written word was terrifying to me. But I have learned that books can travel places that I never will be able to go. And now I get to serve women that I might have never met otherwise. This path of ministry was new, but has been for my good!

Friend, if God is leading you down a new path, you need to trust Him and obey! One of my favorite verses in Proverbs speaks to this command: "Trust in the LORD with all your heart, and do not rely on your own understanding; in all your ways know him, and he will make your paths straight" (Prov. 3:5–6). If you are anything like me, you've likely focused on the first part of that verse—the command to trust God! But this time, focus your eyes on the promise at the end of the verse: God promises our paths will be made straight when we trust the Lord! That is consistent with what Psalm 23:3 describes too: He leads us on paths of righteousness or right, straight paths. In the book of Proverbs, we are told: "There is life in the path of righteousness, and in its path there is no death" (Prov. 12:28). Wow, friend, that's a profound thought: Righteousness is our very life! It reminds me of a hymn I used to sing when I was a little girl: "Then in fellowship sweet, we will sit at his feet. Or we'll walk by his side in the way; what He says we will do; where He sends, we will go. Never fear, only trust and obey. Trust and obey, for there's no other way, to be happy in Jesus, than to trust and obey."[25]

God will lead us on these right paths, but we must follow! We must deny ourselves and our desires for familiarity. Mark 8:34 commands this, "If anyone wants to follow after me, let him deny himself, take up his cross, and follow me." Friends, follow your Shepherd. He knows what is best for your life.

There is a promise tucked onto the end of Psalm 23:3. Did you catch it? These paths are not only for our good, but for His glory! And this is why the psalmist declares, "He leads me along the right paths *for his name's sake*" (Ps. 23:3). When we live and walk with Him, we show the world that we have a Good Shepherd! Our very lives display His goodness. And He gets the honor and the glory for it! The Living Bible says in Psalm 23:3, "He helps me do what honors him the most." When we walk along the right paths, our lives are renewed and restored, and our righteousness brings glory to God. When we let Him lead us, onlookers see Him for who He truly is, and His name is magnified and known in the earth at an ever-greater level than it was before!

Jesus Is Our Righteousness

Jesus doesn't just lead us on these paths of righteousness. The New Testament declares that He is Himself our Righteousness. *Righteousness* is a word that we use a lot in Christian circles, but sometimes we don't even know what it means. Simply put, righteousness is a right standing before God. It is being found holy, perfect, and right in God's eyes. But the problem is that on our own, we are anything but righteous. We are sinful, fallen, and broken people. We have said things we shouldn't say, done things we shouldn't do, wanted things we shouldn't want. The Bible describes us as being dead in our sins. Read Paul's words in Ephesians 2:1–5, with these words italicized:

> And you were *dead* in your trespasses and sins in which you previously walked according to the ways of this world, according to the ruler of the power of the air, the spirit now working in the disobedient. . . . But God, who is rich in mercy, because of his great love that he had for us, made us alive with Christ even though we were *dead* in trespasses. You are saved by grace!

These are familiar verses, but I pray that you don't rush past what they are saying. In these few verses, Paul, describes us as DEAD. Twice! That is what our sin does. It leaves us completely and utterly dead.

In our previous house, we had a huge glass window in the kids' playroom. I remember this one afternoon, a beautiful cardinal flew right into the window with a huge thump. We immediately went outside to see if we could help it, but its sweet neck was broken. No matter how much we tried to straighten its neck or hold it, there was nothing we could do. It was dead. There was no movement. No breathing. No life. No nothing. Just dead.

And did you know that is exactly how we are described in the Bible? Dead in our sins. No eternal life. No future in heaven. Just dead. "But God" (Eph. 2:4). Two of my favorite words in the Bible.

We were walking in disobedience. But God.

We were on paths of destruction. But God.

We were dead. But God.

Because of His great mercy, He made a way for us to be alive with His righteousness. In His great love, He sent Jesus, who was perfect and sinless, to die on the cross for you and for me. On that day, our sin was traded for His righteousness. This is the gospel! This is the good news declared in 2 Corinthians 5:21: "He made the one who did not know sin to be sin for us, so that in him we might become the righteousness of God." By His death on the cross, we have been forgiven and made righteous. We now have right standing before God. First Corinthians 1:30 says, "It is from him that you are in Christ Jesus, who became wisdom from God for us—our righteousness, sanctification, and redemption." Through His death on the cross, not only do we now walk in paths of righteousness, but Jesus Himself *is* our righteousness. And it doesn't stop there! Romans 3:22 declares that "the righteousness of God is through faith in Jesus Christ to all who believe." If you believe this good news, then the righteousness of God can be yours too.

I love that throughout the Bible, clothing is a visual picture of righteousness. When sin entered the world, Adam and Eve knew they were naked and tried to cover themselves with fig leaves. But God. He made a way for them to be clothed with animal skins, by performing the first animal sacrifice. And then, look at what Isaiah 61:10 says about God's covering for His people: "I rejoice greatly in the LORD, I exult in my God; for he has clothed me with the garments of salvation and wrapped me in a robe of righteousness." He trades our nakedness and shame for salvation garments of righteousness. In Revelation, we see clothing once again, as the saints are adorned with robes of white (Rev. 7:9–14)! Jesus is our Righteousness!

Peace in the Renewal and Righteousness of Christ

Friend, what peace we have in Jesus's renewal and righteousness! There is now peace with God. No longer are we enemies, dead in our sins. No longer are we naked and separated from a holy God. In Christ, we are alive and dressed in robes of righteousness. Oh, what grace.

When I think about Jesus as our Righteousness, I realize this also means that we will have peace with others. When we live and walk in these paths of wholeness and goodness, then peace flows in our other relationships too (just like we talked about in chapter 2). When we are found in Christ, the Holy Spirit then begins to produce fruit in our lives like love, joy, peace, patience, kindness, goodness, faithfulness, gentleness, and self-control (Gal. 5:22–23). Perhaps this is why Psalm 85:10b says "righteousness and peace will embrace." When we are living in righteousness, it is the way of peace with God and man.

In Psalm 23:3, David says, "He leads me along the right paths for his name's sake." But look at how similar Psalm 85:13 is to this promise: "Righteousness will go before him to prepare the way for his steps." Our Good Shepherd leads us, goes before us, prepares the way for us . . . with righteousness. He leads us on new paths that are for our good—away from our rutted grooves of destruction. He renews and restores us when we are cast down or stuck in our familiar ways. But most importantly, in Jesus, we find our peace. We trade our sin, sorrow, and shame for His right standing before God. This righteousness is what leads to a life of overflowing peace with God and man. It is not because of anything that we have earned, but it is a gift of God because of His great love and mercy. In Jesus, we find a life of righteousness that leads to overflowing peace. All we must do is trust and obey.

Questions to Consider

1. Have you ever found yourself in a "cast down" state—like you were flat on your back with no way to get back up? Describe what happened and how you felt.

2. Has God ever sheared/pruned a burden from your life? Or has He picked you up and set your feet on solid ground? How has your Shepherd restored you?

3. Are you a creature of habit? Do you like the familiar and the comfortable ways? Why or why not?

4. How has God asked you to trust Him as He has led you down new paths? Even if they were hard, in what ways were these paths for your good and for His glory?

5. When did you first experience the good news that Jesus takes away our sins and gives us His righteousness? How does this righteous living impact your relationship with God and others?

Verses for Reflection

PSALM 40:1–2

I waited patiently for the LORD,
and he turned to me and heard my cry
for help.
He brought me up from a desolate pit,
out of the muddy clay,
and set my feet on a rock,
making my steps secure.

PSALM 56:13

For you rescued me from death,
even my feet from stumbling,
to walk before God in the light of life.

PSALM 37:23–24

A person's steps are established by the
LORD,
and he takes pleasure in his way.
Though he falls, he will not be overwhelmed, because the LORD sup-
ports him with his hand.

PROVERBS 16:9

A person's heart plans his way,
but the LORD determines his steps.

PSALM 5:8

LORD, lead me in your righteousness
because of my adversaries;
make your way straight before me.

The LORD is my shepherd;
I have what I need.

He lets me lie down in green pastures;
he leads me beside quiet waters.

He renews my life;
he leads me along the right paths
for his name's sake.

Even when I go through the darkest valley,
I fear no danger,
for you are with me;
your rod and your staff—they comfort me.

You prepare a table before me
in the presence of my enemies;
you anoint my head with oil;
my cup overflows.

Only goodness and faithful love will pursue me
all the days of my life,
and I will dwell in the house of the LORD
as long as I live.

Psalm 23

Chapter 5

Peace in the Dark Valleys: Our Immanuel

When you were little, were you afraid of the dark? I sure was! I can remember crying most nights and not wanting my mom to leave my room. I would hear a strange noise, and then my mind would begin to race! I figured something was hiding under my bed or in my closet.

Did you know there is a word for this? A fear of the dark is called nyctophobia.[26] It comes from the Greek word for "night" and is an intense fear of darkness that can cause anxiety, depression, and sleeplessness. It manifests itself in not wanting to be alone and is most common in children ages six to twelve. Some researchers estimate that almost half (45 percent) of children have an unusually strong fear of some kind, but most have a fear of the dark because of what they can't see.

I don't blame them: Scary things happen in the dark! Did you know that 30 percent of all violent crimes committed by adults happen between 6 p.m. and 11 p.m.?[27] Drinking under the influence and fatal crashes are more likely to happen in the evening as well.[28] And doesn't it always seem like sickness happens at night too? Oh, how many times have I been awakened in the night by a sick child, either with a fever, a stomach bug, or a bad dream? The sound of our bedroom door opening still causes me to sit straight up from sleep, ready to help a child in need.

This fear of darkness dates back to our ancestors, who lived and slept outside. Predators roamed and enemies attacked at night. The night was most dangerous, which led to a fear of the dark. In order to survive, you had to stay awake. Even in Middle East traditions, the night—and especially the moon—was feared because it was believed to bring ailments, like seizures. This is why Psalm 121:6 comforts the Israelites that the "sun will not strike you by day, or the moon by night." (And in both Matthew 4:24 and 17:15 this "moonstruck" phenomenon—translated as "having seizures"—is mentioned too. Even our English word *lunatic* comes from the base word *lunar*, or "moon"!) A fear of the dark has been around for centuries.

Dark Valleys Are Inevitable

God, in His kindness, speaks right into our fear of darkness in the next verse of Psalm 23. Listen to the comforting words found in verse 4: "Even when I go through the darkest valley, I fear no danger." Or maybe you memorized it in the King James Version: "Yea, though I walk . . ." Whatever translation you read, notice that the psalmist doesn't say "if" I go through the valley, but rather "when" or "yea" (also meaning "yes"). Friend, dark valleys are inevitable for all of us.

David recorded these words because he knew firsthand the difficulties and dangers found in "the darkest valley." It is a real, historical place in the Judean wilderness, called Wadi Qilt. The valley lies between Bethlehem and Judea and originated centuries ago along a freshwater stream. However, during heavy rainfalls, torrents of rushing water from hillsides created a deep and narrow riverbed. Sudden storms and flash floods continued to rampage down the slopes and fill this deep and dark crevice with dangerous waters. When the waters receded, it left behind a narrow and deep valley that has twists and turns. There are parts of it that remain dark even at noon, in the middle of the day. If you ever get a chance to go to Israel, you can visit the Wadi Qilt and see its dark crevices still today. It truly is as David described: the "darkest valley."

David, as a shepherd boy, would have been very familiar with the Wadi Qilt. This dark valley that spans twenty-three miles drops from 2,700 feet in elevation near Jerusalem all the way to Jericho, which is 850 feet below sea level.[29] This valley was useful for moving flocks from the highlands near Bethlehem to the lowlands near Jericho during the winter months. Then, during the spring and summer months, shepherds would travel along the valley again, taking their sheep back to the highlands. David would have traversed this valley many times with his father's flock.

But there are several translations that just don't translate Psalm 23:4 as "the darkest valley." They add in another descriptive word: "valley of the shadow of death" (NKJV and ESV). This is because in the dark valley, death often loomed. Predators hid in the crevices ready to attack the sheep. Enemies would conceal themselves in the darkness and try to attack or rob those passing by. And if a sudden rainstorm hit, the valley would become filled with rushing waters. If a flash flood filled the Wadi Qilt, death would ensue.

As I'm writing this chapter, parts of our country have just experienced a rare "1000-year flood." Hurricane Helene was a Category 4 hurricane that struck the coast of Florida and then traveled up the east coast of the United States in September 2024. Rivers and streams in the mountains of Western North Carolina and Tennessee were overtaken after days of record rainfall. Water rushed off the mountainsides, filling the streams and creek beds to overflowing capacity. This caused mudslides and terrible flooding, with many losing their homes, cars, companies, and possessions. As I've seen footage from these beautiful mountains, I have witnessed what torrential rains and floods can do. These unexpected storms wreaked havoc and many were unable to escape. The total death count has not been released yet, but I imagine it will be in the hundreds. Even in our own country and time period, we know what it is for peaceful valleys to become valleys of death.

Ever since the fall in Genesis 3, death has become part of our existence on this earth. God warned Adam and Eve that if they disobeyed His good commands: "You will certainly die" (Gen. 2:17). That's because to turn away and disobey God is to turn away from life itself. When we sin, we turn from life to death. Listen to the warning of Romans 6:23, "For the wages of sin is death." In other words, what we earn with our sin is death. Death is the natural and only result of turning away from God, who is our life.

God's Word says that death will inevitably come to us all. Romans 5:12 says it this way, "Therefore, just as sin entered the world through one man, and death through sin, in this way death spread to all people, because all sinned." And though our years on earth seem long, the Bible describes our life like steam. James 4:14 warns us, "You do not know what tomorrow will bring—what your life will be! For you are like vapor that appears for a little while, then vanishes." Death is certain. Fallen life is fragile.

I learned this truth firsthand in January 2017. My husband, Jamie, had just returned home from a work trip. He woke up one Saturday morning, hemorrhaging from his large intestine. After being rushed by ambulance to the emergency room, the doctors confirmed that he had an intermittent intestinal bleed. (Praise the Lord that it would start but then stop bleeding. If it hadn't, he would have died after just 3 minutes of bleeding like that!) They tried to stop the bleeding with different procedures for over a week, but nothing worked. He received nine blood transfusions and spent six days in the ICU, getting weaker and weaker from the loss of blood. There were a couple of times he said "goodbye" to me, not knowing if he would make it. Finally, a CT scan determined that the bleed was coming from a weakening in his intestinal lining and the surgeon removed fifteen inches of his large intestine. However, the days that followed abdominal surgery were painful and intense, and he ended up with an infection in his abdomen that required drains and heavy antibiotics. It would be almost a month before we were released to go home. Those are still some of the darkest and heaviest days, when I prepared myself to become a widowed mother of four young children.

I'm so thankful that God protected my husband's life as we walked through that dark valley, but living on planet Earth means that none of us are immune from the taste of death. Whether it comes to us or to someone we love, a dark valley of death is inevitable. When my husband was a pastor, he did more than fifty funerals in the nine years we were there. His first funeral was just a week after he was made the pastor for a church member who died in a car accident. The day we brought our twins home from the hospital, he was called away to care for a family whose son took his own life. Jamie did numerous funerals where we celebrated the life of those who died from old age, heart attacks, or lung conditions. But the worst funeral he ever had to officiate was for a two-year-old little boy who died from brain cancer. His nine-month battle was horrific and though we prayed that God would heal him, He didn't answer our prayers with earthly healing. In just my lifetime, I have lost two great-grandparents, four grandparents, my father, my mother-in-law, and my father-in-law as well. This doesn't count the uncles, cousins, and grandparents on Jamie's side of the family. Our family has walked through the valley of the shadow of death. I'm sure you have your own story of the dark valleys of death too.

Life is indeed fragile, but don't miss the hope tucked into Psalm 23:4. This verse includes an important preposition, which shows movement through a situation. In other words, God promises that we will not stay in the valley of death. We will get *through* it. I have italicized this keyword in a couple different translations or paraphrases so that you can see it for yourself:

> "Even when I go *through* the darkest valley . . ." (CSB)
>
> "Yea, though I walk *through* the valley of the shadow of death . . ." (NKJV)
>
> "Even though I walk *through* the darkest valley . . ." (NIV)
>
> "Even though I walk *through* the valley of the shadow of death . . ." (ESV)

> "Even when the way goes *through* Death Valley . . ." (MSG)
>
> "Even when walking *through* the dark valley of death . . ." (TLB)

Yes, dark valleys are inevitable, but you will get through them. Though they are scary and dark and sometimes filled with circumstances that can kill you, you will not stay there. God will see you through. I love God's promises to Israel in Isaiah 43:1–2 where this same preposition is promised: "Do not fear, for I have redeemed you; I have called you by your name; you are mine. I will be with you when you pass *through* the waters, and when you pass *through* the rivers, they will not overwhelm you. You will not be scorched when you walk *through* the fire, and the flame will not burn you."

Friend, I do want to tell you that sometimes passing through earthly trials doesn't look like we think it will. We aren't guaranteed survival in the earthly sense. We aren't promised healing on this fallen version of earth. We aren't promised if we will get through the valley on this side of eternity or not. Sometimes our healing is only found on the other side of eternity. But that doesn't diminish the fact that God walks alongside us through the darkest valleys of death. We are promised His presence in the valley. Just like the darkest valley in Psalm 23, God notes that when these trials come, you will walk *through* them. And you will not walk alone. God promises, "I will be with you" (Isa. 43:2).

Take Comfort, the Shepherd Is with You

That's the secret to Psalm 23:4, "Even when I go through the darkest valley, I fear no danger, *for you are with me*." Yes, we all experience dark valleys where it is hard to see how to keep going. We all might even know the sting of death and the loss of someone we love. But why can we fear no danger? Why do we not need to be afraid? It's because HE IS WITH US.

The psalm takes a distinct turn here. Up to this point, David has spoken *of* the Lord, but now he speaks *to* the Lord. What was a statement of the Lord as His shepherd, now becomes an intimate dialogue of affection. He begins to use a personal pronoun. "Even when I go through the darkest valley, I fear no danger, for *you* are with me" (v. 4).

The entire psalm climaxes at this verse. To help you picture it, Psalm 23 is kind of like a ladder. Verses 1–3 are on one side, with verses 5–6 on the other side. At the top of the ladder, where it all hinges, is verse 4. The psalm builds to this point and every truth that is shared comes from this one truth: The Lord is my shepherd, and I can have peace because *You are with me.* I can face new paths because *You are with me.* I can lay down and rest because *You are with me.* I can follow Your lead because *You are with me.* Friend, to have a life of overflowing peace, remember this truth: God is with you!

About two months after Jamie and I came home from the hospital in 2017, he asked me a question: "Tara, were you afraid?" As I thought about how to answer, I was torn. On one hand, I was terribly afraid as I processed the "what-ifs." What would life be like without my husband? How would I make ends meet and care for four young children? Where would I work? Where would we live? What if this was the end of his life? But on the other hand, I experienced an unusual peace. I knew that Jamie was saved, and I would see him again in heaven. I didn't know the answers to these logistical questions, but I knew that the same God who provided for me before would provide for us again. And His presence was so real in that hospital room. Jamie said that he was never afraid. He could sense that Jesus was with him and that He would be with me. At the time, neither of us knew the outcome. But we knew God was indeed with us in that dark valley of 2017.

In 2019, I experienced God's presence through another dark valley in my life. I got a phone call that my dad had been taken by ambulance to Duke Hospital, a major medical center in North Carolina. He had been battling multiple myeloma, which is a blood cancer, for more than nine years. He had endured two stem-cell transplants, chemotherapy, radiation, and multiple surgeries. He had gone from being a successful working businessman to being unable to drive or sit for long periods of time. There was even a month when he was bedridden due to the intense pain in his torso and legs. But over that April weekend of 2019, he had stopped being able to walk, couldn't form complete sentences and was not making sense when he spoke. After a week of hospitalization and extensive tests, the doctors confirmed that the cancer had invaded his spinal cord fluid and brain. We were nearing the end of his life, yet he wasn't even seventy years old. He had young married children. He had young grandchildren. This is not how we envisioned his retirement years, and certainly didn't think Mom would be left as a widow in her sixties. We moved my dad into a hospice house, and once again I experienced God's peace and presence with us. My dad was a man of immense faith, and even in those last days, he had a peace that passed all understanding, and so did we. I clung to this truth in Psalm 116:15, "The death of his faithful ones is valuable in the LORD's sight." God was with us and walked with us through that darkest valley.

Friend, your Shepherd, Jesus Christ, has conquered death once and for all! Cherish this promise found in 1 Corinthians 15:54–55, 57: "Death has been swallowed up in victory. Where, death, is your victory? Where, death, is your sting? . . . But thanks be to God, who gives us the victory through our Lord Jesus Christ!" Our God conquered death. Sin and death no longer have the last word. We have victory and eternal life, because of Jesus's death on the cross!

We have a Shepherd who has defeated death. We have a Shepherd who promises to be with us always. His presence is with us in the valley. He is with us on the mountaintop. And He has made a way for us to be with Him forever in the new heavens and new earth. Remember that He is the Good, Great, and Chief Shepherd! He will never leave us! Friend, He will never leave you.

One of my favorite Old Testament passages that exhibits this truth is the story of Joshua. After Moses's death, he led the Israelites from the wilderness, across the Jordan River, and into the Promised Land. Even though he was the leader of this great nation, I can only imagine the fears and insecurities he faced. How could he be the one to lead these people into the Promised Land? Why was he the one chosen to succeed Moses? After all, Moses was a man "whom the LORD knew face to face" (Deut. 34:10). Yet, God had chosen Joshua. And He promised Joshua time and time again that He would be with him. Look at these verses from Joshua 1:

> "I will be with you, just as I was with Moses. I will not leave you or abandon you. Be strong and courageous. . . . Above all, be strong and very courageous. . . . Haven't I commanded you: be strong and courageous? Do not be afraid or discouraged, for the LORD your God is with you wherever you go." . . . "Certainly, the LORD your God will be with you, as he was with Moses." (vv. 5–7, 9, 17)

What a beautiful promise to a new, young leader! He could be strong and courageous because God was with him, no matter what!

God repeated these same truths centuries later to the people through the prophet Haggai. After starting to rebuild the temple, they had stopped. And after sixteen years, Haggai is reminding the people that it's time to get going. Just as God was with them when they conquered the land of Canaan, He was going to be with them as they rebuilt the temple. Listen to these words from Haggai 2:4–5 and see their similarity to Joshua 1:

> "Even so, be strong, Zerubbabel—this is the LORD's declaration. Be strong, Joshua son of Jehozadak, high priest. Be strong, all you people of the land—this is the LORD's declaration. Work! For I am with you—the declaration of the LORD of Armies. This is the promise I made to you when you came out of Egypt, and my Spirit is present among you; don't be afraid."

Be strong. Don't be afraid. Why? Because God was with them! The same beautiful promise is true for us today as believers. No matter what we are facing, we do not need to be afraid because He is with us! Friend, cling to these promises from Psalm 23:4 and Hebrews 13:5–6: "For he himself has said, 'I will never leave you or abandon you.' Therefore, we may boldly say, 'The Lord is my helper; I will not be afraid.'"

Jesus Is Our Immanuel

Remember, a shepherd is always with his sheep. They stay with their flock, all the time. They guide them by walking with them. They dwell with them, so much so that they begin to smell like the sheep. They protect them and provide for them. Close proximity to the shepherd is a key defining difference between a shepherd of sheep and other animals, like horses, cattle, or goats. And close proximity to our Good Shepherd is a key difference between Christianity and other religions too!

One of my favorite names for God is Immanuel, which means "God is with us." We celebrate this name most often at Christmastime because this is the name Mary gave to Jesus when He was born. Matthew 1:23 says, "See, the virgin will become pregnant and give birth to a son, and they will name him Immanuel, which is translated 'God is with us.'" But, my friend, this profound truth is not just to be celebrated on December 25. This truth should impact each day of our lives, even the mundane ones in the middle of the week. Yes, the same Immanuel that we celebrate at Christmas is with you in the middle of the rainy days of March or the hot ones of June. He is Immanuel, God with you!

The God of heaven humbled Himself and came to earth as a little baby. Through the Incarnation, our God dwelt bodily with us, prophesied centuries before: "For a child will be born for us, a son will be given to us, and the government will be on his shoulders. He will be named Wonderful Counselor, Mighty God, Eternal Father, Prince of Peace" (Isa. 9:6). Those four names embody Immanuel. He is our God. He reveals our Father. He is our Counselor. *He is our Peace.*

Because of who He is, we do not need to be afraid. No matter how long the valley might seem. No matter the health diagnosis you or a family member was given. No matter the unexpected loss of someone you love. No matter what dark circumstance you are experiencing. He is there. Do you remember the story of Shadrach, Meshach, and Abednego who were thrown into the fiery furnace? And yet there were "four men, not tied, walking around in the fire unharmed; and the fourth looks like a son of the gods" (Dan. 3:25). Your Shepherd is Immanuel, and with Him, you are never alone.

You can have a life of overwhelming peace, not because of anything you have done but because of who He is and His presence with you. Because He is Immanuel, nothing can separate you from His love. This is what Romans 8:35–39 teaches us:

> Who can separate us from the love of Christ? Can affliction or distress or persecution or famine or nakedness or danger or sword? . . . No, in all these things we are more than conquerors through him who loved us. For I am persuaded that neither death nor life, nor angels nor rulers, nor things present nor things to come, nor powers, nor height nor depth, nor any other created thing will be able to separate us from the love of God that is in Christ Jesus our Lord.

Affliction. Distress. Persecution. Famine. Nakedness. Danger. Sword. Death. Life. Angels. Rulers. Present. Future. Heights. Depths. No created thing. NOTHING can separate you from the love and presence of your God. He is your Shepherd. He is Immanuel, and you do not need to fear because HE IS WITH YOU.

Peace in Immanuel's Presence

Sheep would have peace when walking through the darkest valley because they knew their shepherd was with them. He would never lead them down a trail that he had not walked before. He would protect them from any impending predators. He would walk beside them even when they could not see where they were going. He was leading them to new pastures in new seasons. They had peace, because they knew their shepherd could be trusted.

The same is true for us as the sheep of our Good Shepherd. As we walk through the valley of the shadow of death, we can trust Him because He is with us. He is leading us to new pastures for new seasons. He has walked this path before and knows what lies ahead of us. He knows everything—past, present, and future. In His presence, we too can have peace.

Jesus knew that we would need this reassurance of His presence. So, on the night before His death, He promised His disciples that He would send the Holy Spirit (also called the Counselor) to not only be *with* them, but *in* them. Listen to His words to the Twelve at the Last Supper: "And I will ask the Father, and he will give you another Counselor to be with you forever. He is the Spirit of truth. The world is unable to receive him because it doesn't see him or know him. But you do know him, because he remains with you and will be in you" (John 14:16–17). And then just a few chapters later, Jesus says that it is better for Him to go so that the Holy Spirit will come:

"Nevertheless, I am telling you the truth. It is for your benefit that I go away, but if I don't go away the Counselor will not come to you. If I go, I will send him to you" (16:7).

Why would Jesus say it is better for Him to go and the Holy Spirit to come? Because the Spirit remains with us and will be in us! You cannot get any closer to God than that! And then He says, "I have told you these things so that in me you may have peace. You will have suffering in this world. Be courageous! I have conquered the world" (16:33). Don't you just love that? Peace in Jesus because He has conquered everything, including death! Doesn't His command to be courageous remind you of Joshua 1? I just love God's Word.

We can have peace, not because there aren't dark valleys in this life, but because He is with us through them all. We talk a lot about the famous Great Commission passage that Jesus gives to His followers right before He ascends into heaven. But pay special attention to the last statement: "Go, therefore, and make disciples of all nations, baptizing them in the name of the Father and of the Son and of the Holy Spirit, teaching them to observe everything I have commanded you. *And remember, I am with you always, to the end of the age*" (Matt. 28:19–20). What did He want His disciples to remember? That life would be easy? That there would be no hard times? That there would never be a dark valley to walk through? No. He wanted them to remember that *He was with them always* . . . to the end of the age! Wow, friend. What a gracious goodbye statement from our Savior! It reiterates exactly what Psalm 23:4 says, "Even when I go through the darkest valley, I fear no danger, for you are with me." He is with us in every situation, every trial, every scare, every disappointment, every frustration, and every dark valley. Over and over, He has proven His faithfulness and care. Because He is Immanuel and He is with you—and even *in* you through the indwelling of His Spirit—you can have a life of overflowing peace.

Questions to Consider

1. When you were little, were you afraid of the dark? What was a recurring fear that you had at nighttime?

2. Have you ever experienced the "darkest valley"? How did God carry you through it?

3. Can you attest to God's presence with you "even though I walk through the valley of the shadow of death" (ESV)? How did you know that He was with you?

4. How does knowing that God is Immanuel impact you today? Why is this an important truth to remember every day, not just at Christmas?

5. In what ways is the level of peace you feel affected by your relationship and closeness with God? In other words, how does the knowledge of His presence give you a life of overflowing peace?

Verses for Reflection

ISAIAH 41:10

Do not fear, for I am with you;
do not be afraid, for I am your God.
I will strengthen you; I will help you;
I will hold on to you with my righteous right hand.

2 CORINTHIANS 1:3–4

Blessed be the God and Father of our Lord Jesus Christ, the Father of mercies and the God of all comfort. He comforts us in all our affliction, so that we may be able to comfort those who are in any kind of affliction, through the comfort we ourselves receive from God.

DEUTERONOMY 31:8

"The Lord is the one who will go before you. He will be with you; he will not leave you or abandon you. Do not be afraid or discouraged."

PHILIPPIANS 2:5–11

Adopt the same attitude as that of Christ Jesus, who, existing in the form of God, did not consider equality with God as something to be exploited. Instead, he emptied himself by assuming the form of a servant, taking on the likeness of humanity. And when he had come as man, he humbled himself by becoming obedient to the point of death—even to death on a cross. For this reason, God highly exalted him and gave him the name that is above every name, so that at the name of Jesus every knee will bow—in heaven and on earth and under the earth—and every tongue will confess that Jesus Christ is Lord, to the glory of God the Father.

1 JOHN 4:4

You are from God, little children, and you have conquered them, because the one who is in you is greater than the one who is in the world.

EZEKIEL 34:11–16

"'For this is what the Lord GOD says: See, I myself will search for my flock and look for them. As a shepherd looks for his sheep on the day he is among his scattered flock, so I will look for my flock. I will rescue them from all the places where they have been scattered on a day of clouds and total darkness. I will bring them out from the peoples, gather them from the countries, and bring them to their own soil. I will shepherd them on the mountains of Israel, in the ravines, and in all the inhabited places of the land. I will tend them in good pasture, and their grazing place will be on Israel's lofty mountains. There they will lie down in a good grazing place; they will feed in rich pasture on the mountains of Israel. I will tend my flock and let them lie down. This is the declaration of the Lord GOD. I will seek the lost, bring back the strays, bandage the injured, and strengthen the weak, but I will destroy the fat and the strong. I will shepherd them with justice."

The LORD is my shepherd;
I have what I need.

He lets me lie down in green pastures;
he leads me beside quiet waters.

He renews my life;
he leads me along the right paths
for his name's sake.

Even when I go through the darkest valley,
I fear no danger,
for you are with me;
your rod and your staff—they comfort me.

You prepare a table before me
in the presence of my enemies;
you anoint my head with oil;
my cup overflows.

Only goodness and faithful love will pursue me
all the days of my life,
and I will dwell in the house of the LORD
as long as I live.

Psalm 23

Chapter 6

Peace in the Rod: Our Comfort and Protection

One of our family's favorite meals is pot roast. I have made it so often that the splattered, stained recipe card is now permanently engraved in my memory. It is a simple meal, but one that is requested almost every week by our family. First, you sauté the onions and carrots until they are a beautiful golden brown. Removing them from the pot, you then sear all sides of the salt-and-peppered chuck roast. In a Dutch oven, the roast is then surrounded with the carrots and onions. Beef broth, bay leaves, and spices top it off. You must cook it for 4–5 hours on low heat to allow the meat to fall apart . . . But don't worry, it smells so good as it is cooking! Then, serve the tender pieces of meat over a plate of rice and smother it in gravy. Is your mouth watering yet? Comfort food at its finest.

What is your family's favorite comfort food? Some families love chicken and dumplings. Others love a hearty pot of vegetable beef soup. Still others might take comfort in fried chicken and mashed potatoes. Or maybe your family orders takeout from a local restaurant. Whatever it is, your family probably has a favorite meal that brings comfort to you!

In Psalm 23:4 the psalmist mentions something that brings comfort to sheep. Listen to the two things mentioned: "your rod and your staff—they comfort me." These tools might not bring comfort in the same way that my pot roast does to my family. But the rod and the staff bring comfort to sheep because the shepherd uses them to guard and protect his sheep. Psalm 23:4 in *The Living Bible* is, "You are close beside me, guarding, guiding all the way." And *The Message* paraphrase of this verse is particularly significant: "I'm not afraid when you walk at my side." A shepherd's presence, with his rod and staff, give peace from predators and peace from disobedience. They are a comfort because they are a defense.

A shepherd never leaves home without his rod and his staff. Because each instrument is so unique, we will take time to consider each one individually. In this chapter, we will focus on the first one that is mentioned: a shepherd's rod. Next, in chapter 7, we will examine a shepherd's staff. But make no mistake: Both of them bring comfort because they bring peace.

A Shepherd's Rod

A shepherd's rod looks like a wooden club. It is made from the trunk and root of a sapling. First, a shepherd carefully digs up the young tree by unearthing the root ball, where the trunk connects to the roots. With a knife, he whittles and carves the root ball until it is a hard, round knob. He turns it over and over in his hand until it fits comfortably in his palm, then cuts the sapling to about two and a half feet in length to make the club. This rod becomes an extension of the shepherd's right arm.

The rod is a club of protection against predators and a club of preservation against sheep themselves. As a shepherd carries it, the rod is a symbol of strength, power, and authority. And when he uses this club, it brings peace to the flock. The rod is his means of protecting and guarding.

Protection Against Predators

After a young shepherd makes his rod, he spends hours learning how to wield it. After all, this is his main weapon of defense against predators that would try to hurt his sheep. Coyotes, wolves, and cougars would be prowling around a moving flock, just looking for one to attack and devour. Therefore, a shepherd must always be on the alert and ready. He must know how to throw his rod in a moment's notice with speed and accuracy, in order to hit the predator and defend his sheep. Or, if an animal snuck up and grabbed one of the sheep, the shepherd would need to use his club in combat.

As a shepherd, David knew the protection that came from a rod. He would have used this defense weapon many times in order to protect his sheep from predators. It was this first-hand experience that gave him the confidence to fight the Philistine Goliath. Listen to his account in 1 Samuel 17:34–37:

> David answered Saul, "Your servant has been tending his father's sheep. Whenever a lion or a bear came and carried off a lamb from the flock, I went after it, struck it down, and rescued the lamb from its mouth. If it reared up against me, I would grab it by its fur, strike it down and kill it. Your servant has killed lions and bears; this uncircumcised Philistine will be like one of them, for he has defied the armies of the living God." Then David said, "The LORD who rescued me from the paw of the lion and the paw of the bear will rescue me from the hand of this Philistine."

I wouldn't want to mess with a shepherd and his rod! David told Saul that he wasn't afraid of the giant because he had used his rod against other enemies, particularly lions and bears. If one grabbed a sheep, he would run after it and strike it with the club to rescue the prey. But if the predator went to attack him, he would use the club to protect himself and kill the wild animal. What bravery! What confidence! What comfort!

In addition to striking the predators, a shepherd would use his rod to beat the straggly brush along a path. By hitting the low bushes, the shepherd protected his sheep from snakes or other dangers that might be hiding along the path. He went before the flock, preparing a peaceful path for them. The shepherd's rod truly brought peace for the sheep.

Throughout Scripture, Satan is the enemy of God's plans and His people. Not surprisingly, since we are God's sheep, Satan is often described with the imagery of a predatory animal, like a snake or a lion. The first time we see him described as a snake is in Genesis 3:1 when he tempts Adam and Eve to eat the fruit: "Now the serpent was the most cunning of all the wild animals that the LORD God had made." Then, we see this same imagery appear again in Revelation 12:9 when he is cast out of heaven: "So the great dragon was thrown out—the ancient serpent, who is called the devil and Satan, the one who deceives the whole world. He was thrown to earth, and his angels with him." And in 1 Peter 5:8, he is described as our enemy again, like a roaring lion: "Be sober-minded, be alert. Your adversary the devil is prowling around like a roaring lion, looking for anyone he can devour."

In addition, Jesus warned His disciples of another enemy, and this time He describes them as wolves. These are false teachers, who draw people away from the true gospel. In Matthew 7:15, Jesus warns, "Be on your guard against false prophets who come to you in sheep's clothing but inwardly are ravaging wolves." These false teachers are deceivers, pretending to be an innocent sheep belonging to the flock, but they really are a predator of the people of God. Jesus knew that false teaching and a false gospel were enemies to His flock of followers.

But just as a shepherd's rod protected the sheep from predators, God is our Protector from Satan and others who would try to harm us. David knew this as well, especially when Saul and others were trying to attack him. He boasts in the protection from his enemies that only came from the Lord. Listen to how he describes his foes:

> **Psalm 7:1–2:** "Lord my God, I seek refuge in you; save me from all my pursuers and rescue me, or they will tear me like a lion, ripping me apart with no one to rescue me."

> **Psalm 17:11–12:** "They advance against me; now they surround me. They are determined to throw me to the ground. They are like a lion eager to tear, like a young lion lurking in ambush."

At times, our enemies do seem like prowling lions, eager to rip us apart and we feel like there is no one to rescue us from their lies, or slander, or evilness. But God is there. He rescues us and protects us! And He promises that the Spirit will be there, giving us the words to say. Jesus encouraged, “Look, I’m sending you out like sheep among wolves. Therefore be as shrewd as serpents and as innocent as doves. . . . Don’t worry about how or what you are to speak. For you will be given what to say at that hour, because it isn’t you speaking, but the Spirit of your Father is speaking through you” (Matt. 10:16–20).

David experienced the power of God’s protection from his enemies and foes. He sang a song of thanksgiving to the Lord after God “rescued him from the grasp of all his enemies and from the grasp of Saul” (2 Sam. 22:1). If you have time, read the whole chapter of 2 Samuel 22, because it is chock-full of praise to God for His protection from David’s enemies! Listen to the end: “God—he grants me vengeance and casts down peoples under me. He frees me from my enemies. You exalt me above my adversaries; you rescue me from violent men” (2 Sam. 22:48–49). David, the young shepherd boy, knew the power of the rod against predators for his sheep. Then, as an older man, he knew the power of God’s protection when others tried to harm him. What peace is found in our Shepherd, the great Protector and Comforter!

Protection Against Disobedience

The shepherd’s rod did more than just protect the sheep from outside predators. A shepherd’s rod was also used to protect a sheep from harming itself! If a sheep was wandering away from the flock, getting too close to a dangerous cliff or approaching poisonous plants, a shepherd would use his rod to protect the sheep from hurting itself. A shepherd would hurl the rod toward the sheep, warning it not to go any further. In timidity, a sheep would scurry back to the flock and away from the danger.

However, there are times when a sheep is stubborn. He will continue to go against what the shepherd commands. He will wander on his old familiar paths and get himself in trouble, time and time and again. Most worrisomely, he will disobey the shepherd's instructions and isolate from the flock. There are competing narratives about the use of the shepherd's rod in these cases. You might have heard some say that shepherds would use their rod to break the sheep's leg, splint it and then carry the sheep on his shoulders until the broken leg was completely healed. But a more historical and accurate picture is that the shepherd would use a leg "brake" to train a disobedient or constantly wayward sheep. A "brake" is a heavy clog or weight that attaches to the animal's leg (which is not broken), keeping the sheep that constantly wanders away in disobedience close to the shepherd. As opposed to truly breaking the leg of the sheep, the brake simply slows the sheep down and does not allow the sheep to get very far away from the shepherd. Then, the sheep will finally be around the shepherd long enough to learn his own name and learn not to be afraid or to run away.[30] Shepherds testify after the brake is removed and the leg is restored to full working order, the sheep that was once the most wayward has become the most responsive and obedient. The shepherd "restores" the sheep (Ps. 23:3 NKJV) and through that restoration process, the sheep learns that he never wants to leave the shepherd's side. This echoes the truth found in Psalm 119:71, "It was good for me to be afflicted so that I could learn your statutes." The rod or brake brings correction and peace.

Oh, how much we are like sheep! We can be stubborn and wayward, can't we? Isaiah 53:6 says, "We all went astray like sheep; we all have turned to our own way." Sometimes we also do what we think is right. We will seek the things of this world, thinking that they will satisfy us. Sometimes we are stubborn and stiff-necked, desiring to continue in sin and idolatry rather than obey what God says to do.

But God, in His kindness to us, disciplines us with His rod of correction. In Proverbs 13:24 we are told that God disciplines us because He loves us: "The one who will not use the rod hates his son, but the one who loves him disciplines him diligently." If God did not love us, He would leave us to our stubborn ways. But because He is the Good Shepherd, He will correct us with His rod. It is a protection against our own selfish ways, and teaches us to stay close to Him.

The New Testament echoes this same truthful reality. Consider the promise found in Hebrews 12:11: "No discipline seems enjoyable at the time, but painful. Later on, however, it yields the peaceful fruit of righteousness to those who have been trained by it." His discipline truly is used to bring peace and righteousness in our lives. No, it is not enjoyable while it is happening, but it is for our good.

What's beautiful is what happens after God disciplines us as His children! Just like a shepherd would "brake" the leg of a sheep, our God sometimes slows us down long enough to learn to hear His voice and learn not to run away from Him. It may feel like we're weighed down, incapacitated, or even limping along, but soon enough, our Shepherd will restore us, and when we emerge, we'll be even more responsive and faithful. Note this restorative promise found in Hosea 6:1, "Come, let's return to the LORD. For he has torn us, and he will heal us; he has wounded us, and he will bind up our wounds." Even though God's discipline is painful, He restores us. Through it, we learn that there is peace in His arms. I love Isaiah 40:11, "He protects his flock like a shepherd; he gathers the lambs in his arms and carries them in the fold of his garment. He gently leads those that are nursing." What a picture of our tender Protector. In His arms, there is correction and healing. In His rod, there is protection from our own stubborn and selfish ways.

Peace in God: Our Protector

The shepherd's rod is a protection from both the outside predators and the inward stubbornness of sheep. Likewise, God is our Protector from enemies and our own disobedience too. God's promise to Isaiah is reassurance for us in this: "Do not fear, for I am with you; do not be afraid, for I am your God. I will strengthen you; I will help you; I will hold on to you with my righteous right hand" (Isa. 41:10). Just as the rod was used as an extension of the shepherd's right hand, God comforts His children with this promise: He will protect us with His righteous right hand too.

Throughout Scripture, we see God protecting His people. In Genesis, God protected Adam and Eve by guarding the way to the Tree of Life so that they could not eat that fruit and live in that sinful state forever. At the end of Genesis, God protected Joseph after he had been sold into slavery and elevated him to second-in-command over all the storehouses of Egypt. In the book of Exodus, God protected Moses's life when his mother placed him in a basket in the Nile River. Later in Exodus, we marvel at God's protection as Moses led the Israelites through the Red Sea on dry ground and away from the Egyptian army. In 1 and 2 Samuel, we see God protect David when Saul was plotting to kill him. In Daniel, we see God's protection of Shadrach, Meshach, and Abednego in the fiery furnace. In the book of Ruth, God protected two widows through a kinsman redeemer. In every book of the Bible, you can see God's hand of protection in some way or another.

Of all these biblical examples, perhaps my favorite story of God's protection is found in the book of Esther. After Queen Vashti upsets her husband the King, there is a decree that all young girls be brought to the king's palace. From these virgins, he would choose a new queen. A young Jewish girl, by the name of Hadassah, enters the king's harem. For twelve months, she was given beauty treatments and after her one night with the King, she wins his favor and is made Queen Esther. However, the king's chief minister, Haman, conjures up an evil plan to annihilate all of the Jewish people. It is then that Queen Esther is encouraged to speak to the king. Her cousin Mordecai's famous words challenged her: "Do not think that because you are in the king's house you alone of all the Jews will escape. For if you remain silent at this time, relief and deliverance for the Jews will arise from another place, but you and your father's family will perish. And who knows but that you have come to your royal position for such a time as this?" (Esther 4:13–14 NIV).

Here we see God's hand of protection twice! First, she could have been killed for coming to the king unsolicited. However, she is willing to die as she intercedes for her people. She says in verse 16: "I will go to the king, even though it is against the law. And if I perish, I perish" (NIV). Yet God protected her and gave her favor to speak to her husband. Second, as Queen Esther reveals Haman's evil plan, God protected His chosen people. She says, "If I have found favor with you, Your Majesty, and if it pleases you, grant me my life—this is my petition. And spare my people—this is my request. For I and my people have been sold to be destroyed, killed and annihilated" (7:3–4 NIV). And he grants her request! The king allows the Jews to assemble and fight back on the day they were to be annihilated. God protected the entire Jewish race, and they still celebrate this protection every year with the Feast of Purim.

God is our Protector indeed. My Nana always quoted Psalm 121. She was a tiny 4'11" woman who was married to an alcoholic. She raised her five sons by herself, as her husband would often be out in bars drinking after work. She pawned much of her jewelry just to make ends meet. It wasn't until I was reading her favorite psalm recently that I realized how many times God's protection is mentioned in these few verses. Maybe that's why she clung to these words so much. I have italicized them here for emphasis:

> I lift my eyes toward the mountains.
> Where will my *help* come from?
> My *help* comes from the Lord,
> the Maker of heaven and earth.
>
> He will not allow your foot to slip;
> your *Protector* will not slumber.
> Indeed, the *Protector of Israel*
> does not slumber or sleep.
>
> The Lord *protects* you;
> the Lord is a shelter right by your side.
> The sun will not strike you by day
> or the moon by night.

> The LORD will *protect* you from all harm;
> he will *protect* your life.
> The LORD will *protect* your coming
> and going both now and forever. (Ps. 121)

How beautiful are those words! God is our Helper and Protector. He does not sleep or slumber. He never leaves His throne. He stays with us, right by our side. Like a shepherd, He is with us day and night. He protects our very lives. He keeps us from harm. He protects our ways, both now and forever. Praise be to our Good Shepherd!

Friend, can you see now why there is peace in His protection? We can have lives of overflowing peace knowing that our Shepherd is with us. His rod is an extension of His right arm and is our comfort. With His rod, He protects us from enemies and outside predators. Just like David killed the lions and the bears, our God protects us from Satan and the false teachers around us. God also protects us from our own disobedience! He disciplines us and binds us, so that we will walk closer to Him. He is a good, good Shepherd.

We can echo the words found in Psalm 18:2, "The LORD is my rock, my fortress, and my deliverer, my God, my rock where I seek refuge, my shield and the horn of my salvation, my stronghold." Did you notice all of those "my" pronouns? David knew firsthand the protection of His Shepherd, and He is our Shepherd too. His rod does comfort me, and there is so much peace from His protection!

Questions to Consider

1. What is something that brings comfort to you? Is it a meal? Or a person? Or a special place?

2. How would a shepherd's rod bring comfort to a sheep?

3. Have you ever experienced God's protection from an enemy or circumstance?

4. In what ways has God protected you from your own self or sinfulness?

5. Which Bible story of God's protection do you like the most? Can you think of others in Scripture that were not mentioned in this chapter whom God protected?

Verses for Reflection

PSALM 56:3–4

When I am afraid,
I will trust in you.
In God, whose word I praise,
in God I trust; I will not be afraid.
What can mere mortals do to me?

PSALM 31

Lord, I seek refuge in you;
let me never be disgraced.
Save me by your righteousness.
Listen closely to me; rescue me quickly.
Be a rock of refuge for me,
a mountain fortress to save me.
For you are my rock and my fortress;
you lead and guide me
for your name's sake.
You will free me from the net
that is secretly set for me,
for you are my refuge.
Into your hand I entrust my spirit;
you have redeemed me, Lord, God of
truth. . . .

You have set my feet in a spacious
place. . . .

How great is your goodness,
which you have stored up for those
who fear you.
In the presence of everyone you have
acted

for those who take refuge in you.
You hide them in the protection of
 your presence;
you conceal them in a shelter
from human schemes,
from quarrelsome tongues.
Blessed be the LORD,
for he has wondrously shown his faithful love to me
in a city under siege.
In my alarm I said,
"I am cut off from your sight."
But you heard the sound of my
 pleading
when I cried to you for help.

Love the LORD, all his faithful ones.
The LORD protects the loyal,
but fully repays the arrogant.
Be strong, and let your heart be
 courageous,
all you who put your hope in the
 LORD.

ROMANS 8:38–39

For I am persuaded that neither death nor life, nor angels nor rulers, nor things present nor things to come, nor powers, nor height nor depth, nor any other created thing will be able to separate us from the love of God that is in Christ Jesus our Lord.

PSALM 46:1–2

God is our refuge and strength,
a helper who is always found in times of trouble.
Therefore we will not be afraid.

JUDE 24–25

Now to him who is able to protect you from stumbling and to make you stand in the presence of his glory, without blemish and with great joy, to the only God our Savior, through Jesus Christ our Lord, be glory, majesty, power, and authority before all time, now and forever. Amen.

JOHN 17:9–15

"I pray for them. I am not praying for the world but for those you have given me, because they are yours. Everything I have is yours, and everything you have is mine, and I am glorified in them. I am no longer in the world, but they are in the world, and I am coming to you. Holy Father, protect them by your name that you have given me, so that they may be one as we are one. While I was with them, I was protecting them by your name that you have given me. I guarded them and not one of them is lost, except the son of destruction, so that the Scripture may be fulfilled. Now I am coming to you, and I speak these things in the world so that they may have my joy completed in them. I have given them your word. The world hated them because they are not of the world, just as I am not of the world. I am not praying that you take them out of the world but that you protect them from the evil one."

The LORD is my shepherd;
I have what I need.

He lets me lie down in green pastures;
he leads me beside quiet waters.

He renews my life;
he leads me along the right paths
for his name's sake.

Even when I go through the darkest valley,
I fear no danger,
for you are with me;
your rod and your staff—they comfort me.

You prepare a table before me
in the presence of my enemies;
you anoint my head with oil;
my cup overflows.

Only goodness and faithful love will pursue me
all the days of my life,
and I will dwell in the house of the LORD
as long as I live.

Psalm 23

Chapter 7

Peace in the Staff: Our Comfort and Rescue

When I was a little girl, our family lived in Florida and had season passes to Walt Disney World. Almost every October, we loaded up in our family's station wagon and headed to "The Happiest Place on Earth." Our favorite place to stay was Fort Wilderness in a little log cabin, nestled among the tall pine trees. Each morning, we would ride the shuttles into the Magic Kingdom. I can still picture the front entrance and the feeling of excitement as Tinker Bell opens the gates and you turn the corner to see Cinderella's castle!

Even though we would try to arrive early and go at the least busy time of year, there were still large crowds of people. Millions of visitors come each year. I was amazed to see all the visitors from other countries too! As a little girl, there were so many people and so many sights to see: characters, store fronts, shows, parades, rides, and food! But if I wasn't careful, it was also easy to get separated from my family.

I vividly remember one time when we had stopped to watch a street show with Chip and Dale. Their antics had me enthralled, but after a few minutes, I turned around and couldn't see my mom or dad. I began to panic. My eyes were searching high and low all around me. I was turning in circles, but I couldn't find them. My heart started beating faster. Where did they go? I was breathing quickly and felt the tears welling up in my eyes. I was lost! People were all around me, but I was alone and separated from my family. But then, all of a sudden, I felt this big arm scoop around me and pick me up. It was my dad! He had told me it was time to go, but I hadn't heard him. After a few steps away, they realized I wasn't there with them, and he came back to get me. I was lost, but then my dad found me. What comfort his arms were to me that day!

A Shepherd's Staff

My dad's strong arm was like the second tool—a shepherd's staff—described in Psalm 23:4. It says, "Your rod and your staff—they comfort me." A shepherd's staff is the most recognizable piece of equipment that identifies a shepherd. This wooden crook is not used by any other profession. A shepherd will never leave home or try to guide their flock without it. If you see a person carrying a staff, you know he or she is a shepherd.

Just like the rod, a shepherd carefully selects a sapling to make his staff. He must first find a young tree that is the perfect length, just one to two feet taller than his height. Then a shepherd will cut the young sapling just above the ground. Unlike with the rod, however, he will not dig up the root ball. Instead, he just uses the trunk of the tree. He selects a young tree that is still green and pliable. After soaking the cut tree in water for a few days to soften it even more, a shepherd will then bend the top to make a hook. He will tie his wooden staff in this position for a few weeks, in order to permanently create the crook. It remains in this tied position until the wood has dried and hardened.[31] When it is fully seasoned, the shepherd will smooth and sand his staff to his personal liking. It must feel good and fit well in his hands because this hook will remain with him wherever he travels with his flock.

In addition to being made from the right material, the staff must be the right size and shape. First, it must be long enough to extend a shepherd's arm in times of need. However, it must not be so long that it is unable to be wielded or used by the shepherd. In addition, the crook must be big enough to fit around a lamb's chest, but small enough that it doesn't slip off when it's used to pick the lamb up. In addition, it must be able to fit around a bigger sheep's neck without strangling it but fit snuggly enough that it can rescue an endangered sheep. The staff must be just the right length and width.

Of all the tools he uses, the staff is the essential and gentle reminder of a shepherd's comfort. With it, a shepherd can restore a straying sheep. He can guide a flock along the paths using his staff. It can push branches away so that sheep can travel through thorny passages. The staff gives steadiness when a shepherd is walking along steep hills. Or a shepherd can lean on it for support and strength. When a sheep has gotten entangled, the crook is used to rescue. The shepherd's staff is the ultimate symbol of love. That is why David says it "comforts" him (Ps. 23:4).

The Rescuing Staff

I'm sure you have heard the famous line from J. R. R. Tolkien, "Not all who wander are lost."[32] However, that is not the case with sheep. They are susceptible to wandering and most definitely will get lost. They will stray away from the protection of the shepherd and can find themselves in predicaments that aren't good. Therefore, the shepherd's staff is most used in rescuing a lost or entangled sheep.

Because sheep are not very smart, they will just follow their noses, nibbling and grazing on any green grass they can find. This often leads them to stray quite far from the flock without even realizing it. A shepherd's eyes are constantly roaming over his flock. When he sees one that is wandering too far, he will use his staff to guide the sheep back in the right direction, in order to be restored to the rest of the flock.

Jesus even taught about this in His "Parable of the Lost Sheep." In Luke 15:4–7, Jesus is questioned by the Pharisees about why He seeks out sinners. After all, why does He want to dine with sinful, lost, broken people? Jesus replies with the beautiful heart of a Shepherd, who always seeks out the lost sheep:

> "What man among you, who has a hundred sheep and loses one of them, does not leave the ninety-nine in the open field and go after the lost one until he finds it? When he has found it, he joyfully puts it on his shoulders, and coming home, he calls his friends and neighbors together, saying to them, 'Rejoice with me, because I have found my lost sheep!' I tell you, in the same way, there will be more joy in heaven over one sinner who repents than over ninety-nine righteous people who don't need repentance."

A shepherd will always go to find his lost sheep, because he loves his sheep. Knowing that his sheep can be careless and can wander too far without realizing it, a shepherd will use his staff to rescue the sheep that has separated from the group. In the same way, Jesus rescues us as sinners when we are separated from God. I love the words of the old hymn:

"Amazing grace, how sweet the sound. That saved a wretch like me! I once was lost, but now I'm found. Was blind but now I see."[33] What comfort our Good Shepherd is to us with His staff of rescue!

In addition to being careless and wandering, sheep can be very clumsy. Their hooves can slip easily on rocky surfaces. This causes them to lose their balance often. In just a second or two, a sheep can fall from a flat surface into a ravine or deep crevice. Then, there is no way for them to get back up to where they are supposed to be. Sheep are not good climbers and will just stumble and fall back down. When this happens, you will hear sheep bleating and bleating for help. Just as a shepherd's eyes are roaming across his grazing flock, his ears are open for those who need him. A sheep is lost until the shepherd hears and comes to find them. In this case, a shepherd knows that the sheep doesn't need the rod of discipline. The sheep wasn't acting out of disobedience, like we talked about in the last chapter. They are just mistaken and clumsy. What they need is a staff of rescue to lift them up from the place where they are stuck.

This reminds me of the beautiful verses in Psalm 40:1–2, when David testifies of God's goodness in helping him when he was stuck. David says, "I waited patiently for the Lord, and he turned to me and heard my cry for help. He brought me up from a desolate pit, out of the muddy clay, and set my feet on a rock, making my steps secure." Friend, aren't you and I so prone to falling, just like sheep? We get stuck in pits or stranded in the muddy clay of our mistakes, and no matter what we do, we can't get out. But then God, in His mercy and grace, rescues us and sets our feet back on solid ground.

Sheep can get stuck in other places, not just ravines, pits, or mud. Because they are covered in curly wool, their fleece can easily get stuck in their surroundings. As they are grazing with their noses to the ground, they might not even realize that they are near a thorny brush or prickly patch. In no time, their wool can get hooked on these thorns or thistles. This causes the sheep to be entangled, and the more they struggle to set themselves free, the more entrapped they become. Quickly, they will be unable to move as their wool coat is entangled completely. A shepherd who has been keeping watch over his flock will come to the trapped sheep's rescue! He will use his staff to dislodge the sheep and pull it to safety.

Like sheep, we cannot save ourselves from the predicaments we find ourselves in. The author of Hebrews describes the trappings of this world as something that "so easily entangles" (Heb. 12:1 NIV). Just as a shepherd, with his loving staff, will never give up on the lost and careless sheep, God promises to rescue us too! I love the promises of Isaiah 41:13, "For I am the LORD your God, who holds your right hand, who says to you, 'Do not fear, I will help you.'" What good news! Our God will come to our rescue and help us! And then we can echo the truths of 2 Corinthians 12:9, when Jesus told the apostle Paul, "My grace is sufficient for you, for my power is perfected in weakness." Jesus knows that we are weak. And yet, He will help us! His grace is sufficient for us and His shepherd's staff rescues us. What comfort!

The prophet Nehemiah recounts God's mercy and love as a rescuing Shepherd in one of my favorite verses in the Old Testament. He describes how God rescued the Israelites from the Egyptians and was even patient with their fallings in the wilderness. He then sums up God's nature toward us in this one verse: "But you are a forgiving God, gracious and compassionate, slow to anger and abounding in faithful love, and you did not abandon them" (Neh. 9:17). Don't you just love all of those attributes of God in that one tiny verse? Just like a shepherd will never give up on a lost, careless, clumsy or entangled sheep, God will not abandon us. He is forgiving. He is gracious. He is compassionate and long-suffering. The shepherd's staff of rescue is the ultimate picture of God's steadfast and faithful love. It truly is our comfort.

The Guiding Staff

A shepherd's staff is not only used to rescue a lost or entangled sheep. It is also the tool by which a shepherd affectionately guides his flock. He will place the tip of the crook along a sheep's side, guiding them to travel along a new path. This is why *The Living Bible* paraphrases Psalm 23:4, ". . . for you are close beside me . . . guiding all the way."

God is often described in Scripture as a shepherd, guiding His people like sheep, with His staff in hand. Psalm 78:52–53 speaks of God leading the Israelites out of Egypt: "He led his people out like sheep and guided them like a flock in the wilderness. He led them safely, and they were not afraid." After they were freed from Egypt, God led them in the desert with a pillar of fire by night and a cloud by day. His visible presence guided them in the wilderness in the same way that a shepherd's staff would guide the flock! Once the people had crossed through the dry ground of the Red Sea, Moses led the people in singing a song to God, praising Him for being their guide: "With your faithful love, you will lead the people you have redeemed; you will guide them to your holy dwelling with your strength" (Exod. 15:13). A few centuries later, God reminds the people again that He is their Shepherd who will not leave them. Through the prophet Isaiah, God reiterates that He will guide them: "I will lead the blind by a way they did not know; I will guide them on paths they have not known. I will turn darkness to light in front of them and rough places into level ground. This is what I will do for them, and I will not abandon them" (Isa. 42:16). What a wonderful promise! God will lead us and never abandon us, just as a shepherd would never abandon His sheep.

But, friend, it gets better. As Christians, we now have the Holy Spirit as our Guide! As we discussed in a previous chapter, Jesus told His disciples that it was better for Him to ascend to heaven so that the Holy Spirit would come to us (John 16:7).

He promised that God "will give you another Counselor to be with you forever. He is the Spirit of truth. . . . He remains with you and will be in you" (John 14:16–17). The Holy Spirit of God dwells inside of each of us, to lead, guide and direct us. He is our Counselor, reminding us of Jesus's words (v. 26), teaching us, and is the one who "will guide you into all the truth" (16:13). And so perhaps this is why Jesus says, "Peace I leave with you. My peace I give to you. I do not give to you as the world gives. Don't let your heart be troubled or fearful" (14:27). Jesus knew that if He left, the Holy Spirit would come. And He is our peace—as He leads and guides us, just like a shepherd's staff.

The Affectionate Staff

I love that the shepherd's staff is not just used to rescue and guide the sheep. It is also used to show affection. A shepherd will use his staff to walk "hand in hand" with a sheep, by placing the staff around the sheep as they walk beside each other. It is a comforting presence, almost as if they are holding hands, or perhaps as if the sheep senses an arm around its shoulder, as they are walking. But what an affectionate way to guide and lead his sheep! This is why *The Message* translates Psalm 23:4 as "Your trusty shepherd's crook makes me feel secure."

The shepherd's staff, when used in this way, is a symbol of God's faithful love for His people. His is a steadfast love that seeks, forgives, reconciles, restores, and leads. Just like there is no ravine, no thorny brush, no ditch that can separate a shepherd from his sheep, there is nothing that can separate us from the love of our Shepherd! Listen to Jesus's promise in John 10:27–28: "My sheep hear my voice, I know them, and they follow me. I give them eternal life, and they will never perish. No one will snatch them out of my hand." The shepherd's staff truly brings comfort, because nothing can separate us—or snatch us—from the faithful love of our God!

When we receive His love, there is no other response than to praise. We are loved by the Almighty Creator of heaven and earth! We are loved by the One who knows us perfectly and loves us anyway! We are loved by the Savior, Rescuer, and Redeemer who guides us with His own staff to keep us close to Him forevermore! Therefore, we sing like David: "Give thanks to the Lord, for he is good. His faithful love endures forever. Give thanks to the God of gods. His faithful love endures forever. Give thanks to the Lord of lords. His faithful love endures forever. He alone does great wonders. His faithful love endures forever" (Ps. 136:1–4).

His faithful love endures forever. What a refrain! What an assurance! What a comfort.

God Is Our Comforter

The shepherd's staff is truly the picture of the love and comfort we find in our Good Shepherd. It brings comfort when we find ourselves entangled in sin, because He will rescue and forgive us. It brings comfort when we are down in a pit, because His Word is life and joy. It brings comfort when we don't know which way to go, because His Spirit will guide and direct us. It brings comfort because in all these things, we are promised that nothing can disconnect or take us from the love of our God. Nothing can distance Him from us. Nothing can keep our Shepherd from His sheep. His love is steadfast toward us. What a comfort!

I love the repetition found in 2 Corinthians 1:3–7 about the comfort that we find in God. I have italicized some words for emphasis in this passage. Don't miss the beautiful blessing of being loved by an Almighty God, who is the God of all comfort:

> Blessed be the God and Father of our Lord Jesus Christ, the Father of mercies and the God of all *comfort*. He *comforts* us in all our affliction, so that we may be able to *comfort* those who are in any kind of affliction, through the *comfort* we ourselves receive from God. For just as the sufferings of Christ overflow to us, so also through Christ our *comfort* overflows. If we are afflicted, it is for your *comfort* and salvation. If we are *comforted*, it is for your *comfort*, which produces in you patient endurance of the same sufferings

> that we suffer. And our hope for you is firm,
> because we know that as you share in the sufferings, so you will also share in the *comfort*.

Now remember that in the original text, the authors couldn't bold and italicize words for emphasis. So they would repeat them to grab the attention of their listeners. Do you see how many times the word *comfort* is repeated? In just four verses, Paul writes it nine times! That should perk up our ears! God is the One who comforts us in all our hardships. He is the One who is the God of all comfort. And He promises that when we receive comfort from Christ through our sufferings, it will overflow to others who also need comfort. In other words, when He comforts us, we should comfort others.

If we want to live a life of overflowing peace, then it is not found in anything other than the God of all comfort. Just as a shepherd's staff brought comfort and peace to his flock, so does God's Spirit bring comfort and peace to our hearts. It is by His Spirit that He guides us. It is by His Spirit that He convicts us of sin and rescues us from the pits of our own destruction and the predatory attacks of our enemy. It is by His Spirit that we experience the steadfast love and affection of our God. And it is by His Spirit that we can truly experience peace.

When we are rescued from our sin and our enemy, we find true peace in our Savior. No longer is the curse of death and sin on us. Through Jesus, we have been reconciled and have peace with God. When we experience His steadfast love, we have peace from our loneliness and fears. When we are guided by His Spirit, we can have peace that we are no longer lost and wandering. Our home is in heaven. His shepherd's staff, His Spirit, truly brings us comfort and peace!

Friend, I think we can honestly recite with David, "Your rod and your staff—they comfort me" (Ps. 23:4). These two tools—which a shepherd always carries with him—are the ultimate sign of comfort and peace. With them, a sheep is defended and protected. With them, a sheep is lovingly guided and rescued. Knowing that we belong to a Good Shepherd should reassure us that His rod and His staff truly lead to a life of overflowing peace.

Questions to Consider

1. Have you ever been lost? Describe the time and how you felt.

2. Are you a wanderer? Have you ever had God's staff rescue you when you strayed too far?

3. Has there been a time in your life when you felt stuck or entangled in something you couldn't get out of? How did God rescue you in that season?

4. In what ways does God guide you in life? How does He use His Word or the Holy Spirit to lead and direct you?

5. When has God's Spirit comforted you? How did it bring peace to your heart in that situation?

Verses for Reflection

LUKE 1:78–79

> "Because of our God's merciful compassion, the dawn from on high will visit us to shine on those who live in darkness and the shadow of death, to guide our feet into the way of peace."

PSALM 103:11–14

For as high as the heavens are above
the earth,
so great is his faithful love
toward those who fear him.
As far as the east is from the west,
so far has he removed
our transgressions from us.
As a father has compassion on his
children,
so the LORD has compassion on those
who fear him.
For he knows what we are made of,
remembering that we are dust.

JOHN 16:33

"I have told you these things so that in me you may have peace. You will have suffering in this world. Be courageous! I have conquered the world."

ISAIAH 43:1–2 (NIV)

"Do not fear, for I have redeemed you;
I have summoned you by name; you
are mine.
When you pass through the waters,
I will be with you;
and when you pass through the rivers,
they will not sweep over you.
When you walk through the fire,
you will not be burned;
the flames will not set you ablaze."

PSALM 16:8

I always let the LORD guide me.
Because he is at my right hand,
I will not be shaken.

The Lord is my shepherd;
I have what I need.

He lets me lie down in green pastures;
he leads me beside quiet waters.

He renews my life;
he leads me along the right paths
for his name's sake.

Even when I go through the darkest valley,
I fear no danger,
for you are with me;
your rod and your staff—they comfort me.

You prepare a table before me
in the presence of my enemies;
you anoint my head with oil;
my cup overflows.

Only goodness and faithful love will pursue me
all the days of my life,
and I will dwell in the house of the Lord
as long as I live.

Psalm 23

Chapter 8

Peace in the Table: Our Satisfaction

When I was growing up, my mom always decorated our kitchen table for special holidays. My siblings and I would come downstairs in the morning before school to find a beautiful table prepared for us! I can remember how she would set it for our birthdays, complete with streamers, balloons, and presents filling the table of celebration! For Valentine's Day, Mom always used a pink tablecloth and scattered little conversation hearts all over it, with other chocolate candy boxes at our places. Christmas morning was always the most special! We would come downstairs to find the table covered in a red tablecloth, with her fancy China plates set at each spot, and a birthday cake for Jesus in the middle.

This is a tradition that I now continue with my own children. I stay up after they've all gone to bed to create a special table for the next day. That way, as soon as they wake up in the morning, they can walk into the kitchen and find a table that has been set for them. I use different color tablecloths, special plates, decorations, and centerpieces for each holiday, and my kids really love it! I hope one day they will continue this tradition with their own kids.

A Table Prepared for Us

In Psalm 23, starting in verse 5, there is additional insight provided in the shepherding metaphor. The shepherd is still the Good Shepherd as depicted in verses 1–4, but He's also pictured as the Host of a banquet table. Verse 5 says, "You prepare a table before me . . ." Now, this table is not like the table that I create for my kids or like the ones my mom created for me. But it is true that your heavenly Father has prepared a table for you.

First let's see this in reference to a shepherd's table. They had to provide green pastures for their sheep, like we discussed earlier in chapter 2. To have pastures of green grass, a shepherd needed to go before his flock and plant fields for them to graze in. This typically happened in the spring, months before their sheep would need it. Shepherds would venture to these remote, harder-to-reach altitudes and prepare the field for them. Then, after a month or two, he would lead his flock back up to these high ranges because the newly sprouted green pastures were perfect for the sheep to graze in during the hotter months of the summer. In English, we call these plateaus "mesas." Did you know that *mesa* is the Spanish word for table? So, when a shepherd would prepare the fields for his sheep, he would be preparing the "mesa," or table, for them. It shows that the shepherd was thoughtful to plan and prepare, so that he could provide for the needs of his sheep both in the present, but also in the future.

Alternatively, don't miss the beautiful picture of the table in Psalm 23:5 as a picture of the full satisfaction we find in God as our Host. *The Living Bible* says, "You provide delicious food for me in the presence of my enemies." *The Message* paraphrases it as "You serve me a six-course dinner." Just as a sheep would lie down in the green pastures because he was fully content and had all he needed, we have full satisfaction in God's table too. He even used this language when telling His people about the Promised Land: "I will provide rain for your land in the proper time, the autumn and spring rains, and you will harvest your grain, new wine, and fresh oil. I will provide grass in your fields for your livestock. You will eat and be satisfied. Be careful that you are not enticed to turn aside, serve, and bow in worship to other gods" (Deut. 11:14–16). Did you see that second sentence that describes grass and being fully satisfied? God is a Good Shepherd and Gracious Host to His people! Psalm 145:15–16 describes this same concept: "All eyes look to you, and you give them their food at the proper time. You open your hand and satisfy the desire of every living thing."

From Genesis to Revelation, we see images of God's people being fully satisfied, as they feasted at His table and the food He provided. It began in the garden of Eden, where Adam and Eve had every type of fruit, seed, and plant that they desired (Genesis 1–2). In Exodus, we see God institute the Passover meal, prepared with lamb and unleavened bread (Exodus 12). Even in the wilderness, God provided manna and quail as a daily table set for them each day (Exod. 16:8). In the tabernacle, we see the Table of Showbread with the "Bread of the Presence on the table before me at all times," reminding the people how God provides for their daily bread (Exod. 25:30).

God provided for His people time and time again. For Jacob and his sons, God provided grain through the storehouses of Egypt (Genesis 47). For the Levites, God provided grain, oil, and wine (Deut. 18:4). For Elijah, God provided bread and meat, brought by the ravens (1 Kings 17:5–6). For Ruth, God provided wheat through Boaz's fields (Ruth 2:8–9). For Mephibosheth, God provided food through the table of King David (2 Sam. 9:7–9). For the widow, God provided oil (2 Kings 4).

These images continue in the New Testament, where Jesus displayed how God satisfies us with food during His earthly ministry too. He feeds 5,000 men, not counting the women and children, with just two fish and five loaves of bread that

He multiplied! There was so much leftover that it filled twelve baskets (Matt. 14:13–21). Talk about eating until you are satisfied and there still being an abundance! This was not the only miracle that is recorded in which Jesus set the table for thousands (Mark 8:1–10). Jesus also prepared a Passover meal in the Upper Room for His disciples the night before He was crucified (Matt. 26:17–29). After His resurrection, He cooked fish on the shore of the Sea of Galilee for Simon Peter and the other fishermen (John 21:9).

Even in the early New Testament church, God makes sure that His people have the food provisions that they need. Acts 2 describes how they "held all things in common" and "broke bread from house to house. They ate their food with joyful and sincere hearts" (Acts 2:44–46). When the followers of Jesus were growing in number, some widows were being overlooked in the daily food distribution, but God made sure they were taken care of and selected seven men who would serve the food (Acts 6:1–3). He is a God who provides for our needs, abundantly.

The most beautiful table is found in Revelation where we see another banquet table set. This is at the Marriage Feast of the Lamb, where we will celebrate the final reunion and consummation of Christ and His bride (the saints of the church). It will be the most joyous, fulfilling banquet feast of all, with each place set and every believer invited. He desires for anyone who believes to have a seat at this table. Listen to the words in Revelation 19:7–9a:

> "Let us be glad, rejoice, and give him glory, because the marriage of the Lamb has come, and his bride has prepared herself. She was given fine linen to wear, bright and pure."
>
> For the fine linen represents the righteous acts of the saints.
>
> Then he said to me, "Write: Blessed are those invited to the marriage feast of the Lamb!"

What a glorious, eternal table that will be. It will satisfy the deepest hungers and thirsts of our soul.

My friend, I hope you don't miss this truth: Our God is the One who has been setting tables from Genesis to Revelation. He has always met the physical need of food for His people. However, I want you to know that your Shepherd and Host not only meets your physical needs; He also satisfies every other need we have. Savor the beautiful promises of Philippians 4:19–20, "And my God will supply all your needs according to his riches in glory in Christ Jesus . . ." God supplies *all* our needs. From the riches of Christ, we are fully satisfied in the table of our God both now and forevermore. Physical needs. Emotional needs. Mental needs. Spiritual needs. All our needs are met in the beautiful rich table of our God.

Maybe this is why the psalmist states in Psalm 23:5: "My cup overflows." Our lives are so full, so satisfying that God's peace and goodness run over. In His table, we find an abundance that we cannot keep to ourselves. A life so rich that it spills out to others around us. Psalm 16:5–6 has echoes of these truths as well:

> LORD, you are my portion
> and my cup of blessing;
> you hold my future.
> The boundary lines have fallen for me
> in pleasant places;
> indeed, I have a beautiful inheritance.

God is our satisfaction and portion both today and forever. He satisfies us in this life and in the life to come, holding our future and beautiful inheritance on the table set before us. What a good Shepherd and Host we have!

In the Presence of Enemies

There is an interesting statement at the end of Psalm 23:5: "You prepare a table before me in the presence of my enemies." In the presence of those who are our enemies?! Well, I don't know about you, but I haven't done that in our home for our children!

When a shepherd would go to the high mesas to prepare the pastures for his sheep, he often would do that in the presence of enemies. During those early spring months, as he ventured to the hard-to-reach altitudes, he knew enemies were lurking all around him. Not necessarily human enemies, but various types of wild animals would be hiding in the crevices or lurking to find their next meal. Mountain lions, coyotes, foxes, wolves, and bears were enemies not only for their flocks but also for the shepherds themselves in the days following the winter. With his club in his hand, a shepherd would go to prepare the table knowing enemies were all around him. He would kill or trap as many of the predators as possible, preparing the pasture to be safe for his flock.

Another way that the shepherd prepared the pasture for his flock was by removing poisonous enemies from the mesa, like weeds and contaminated (or stagnant) watering holes. Let's consider first the poisonous weeds. These are literal enemies of the sheep, sprouting up right in the middle of the new grass. The weeds easily blended in with the grass but could be deadly for a grazing flock. So a shepherd would need to rid the pasture of any poisonous weeds before his sheep could graze freely there. Second, a shepherd needed to get rid of the poisonous watering holes. Over the winter months, twigs, branches, and other debris would fall into the water source. This would cause polluted standing water that would be deadly for sheep. In order to prepare the pastures for his flock, a shepherd would get rid of anything in the watering holes that would lead to stagnant, poisonous water. As the shepherd prepared the table, it was in the presence of these two other enemies: weeds and poisonous water.

When Jesus was on earth, He also prepared a table for His people in the presence of enemies. He often would dine with sinners and tax collectors, the very ones who were the enemies of the Jews. Tax collectors were Jewish people who worked for the Romans, stealing extra money from their own people to line their own pockets with profit. Yet Jesus dined with many of them:

> While he was reclining at the table in the house, many tax collectors and sinners came to eat with Jesus and his disciples. When the Pharisees saw this, they asked his disciples, "Why does your teacher eat with tax collectors and sinners?" Now when he heard this, he said, "It is not those who are well who need a doctor, but those who are sick. . . . I didn't come to call the righteous, but sinners." (Matt. 9:10–13)

Perhaps the greatest example of Jesus dining with an enemy however was at the Last Supper. On the night before He was crucified, Jesus prepared a meal for His disciples in the Upper Room. Sitting to His left, in the seat of honor, was Judas. Biblical accounts tell us that they dipped their hands into the same dish (Matt. 26:23). Yet just hours later, Judas would betray Jesus for thirty pieces of silver. A disciple, turned enemy, would reveal his infidelity with a kiss. Knowing all this, Jesus prepared this table and dined in the presence of a betrayer, an enemy.

Not only did Jesus love His enemies, but He commands us to do the same. Listen to Luke 6:27–28: "But I say to you who listen: Love your enemies, do what is good to those who hate you, bless those who curse you, pray for those who mistreat you." His commands are so counter-cultural and unnatural to us. It is our inclination to hate those who hate us and to despise those who mistreat us. Yet Jesus commands something completely opposite. Love those who are our enemies. Bless them. Pray for them. It is in doing so that we experience Jesus's peace at His table. After all we, too, were enemies of God. Romans 5:10 says, "For if, while we were enemies, we were reconciled to God through the death of his Son, then how much more, having been reconciled, will we be saved by his life." In His death, we are reconciled to God. By His wounds, we are given life. We who were enemies now have a seat at His Father's table.

Eternal Peace with God: Our Satisfaction

This leads us to another important meal in the life of a believer. Every time we take the Lord's Supper, or Communion, at church, we are declaring to ourselves that our Shepherd and Host "prepare a table before me in the presence of my enemies" (Ps. 23:5). Just as Judas dined with Him at the table, we too were enemies of God. And yet, Jesus died in our place. He defeated our greatest enemies—Satan and death—for us, and He invites us to His table.

But as the New Testament teaches us, at this table, Jesus is no longer just the Host. He is the meal Himself. Listen to the words of 1 Corinthians 11:23–26 with this in mind: "On the night when he was betrayed, the Lord Jesus took bread, and when he had given thanks, broke it, and said, 'This is my body, which is for you. Do this in remembrance of me.' In the same way also he took the cup, after supper, and said, 'This cup is the new covenant in my blood. Do this, as often as you drink it, in remembrance of me.' For as often as you eat this bread and drink the cup, you proclaim the Lord's death until he comes." We are called to remember His sacrificial death on the cross, and rest in the reminders of this table: Through His substitutionary atonement, we have eternal life.

Friend, remember what He has done when you approach the prepared table of Communion with your local church body. It is at the Lord's Supper Table that we remember the blood that He shed for us and His body that was broken for us. In taking Communion, we are proclaiming that He defeated our greatest enemy and has brought us reconciliation with God. Jesus has made a way for us to be eternally satisfied in God. When we come to the table of the Lord's Supper, we are remembering that at this table He has set for us, we find our peace.

Romans 5:1 contains this truth that we should shout from the top of our lungs. I have italicized three words for emphasis: "Therefore, since we have been justified by faith, we have *peace with God* through our Lord Jesus Christ." Through Jesus's death on the cross, we have been given access to the table of our God—a table set in the presence of enemies. He is our satisfaction, not only for physical needs, but because the wrath of God was satisfied in Christ. He is not only the host, but the satisfying meal. He Himself is our peace.

Friend, we have been given salvation and eternal peace with God. What satisfaction! More than food or even our daily bread, we need the wrath of God to be satisfied toward us, and in Christ, it has been! Therefore, He alone invites you into a life of overflowing peace. Peace in that our penalty of sin has been paid. Peace in that we are right with God. Peace that "runs over" in abundance when we follow Him. We have a Good Shepherd who "prepares a table" before us and invites us to come sit with Him. He is our satisfaction.

Questions to Consider

1. How does a prepared table express planning, thoughtfulness, and love? Have you ever had someone prepare a table for you?

2. We see the theme of food and feasting from Genesis to Revelation. Which images of a "prepared table" in the Old or New Testament resonate with you the most?

3. In what ways does Jesus's example of dining with sinners encourage or challenge you to do the same?

4. Jesus's command to love our enemies is not something that is natural or easy. How do you bless and love those who are your enemy?

5. How can we see communion in a different light? How does this act symbolize the truth of Psalm 23:5, a prepared table in the presence of our enemies?

Verses for Reflection

PSALM 22:26

The humble will eat and be satisfied;
those who seek the LORD will praise
him.
May your hearts live forever!

PSALM 107:9

For he has satisfied the thirsty
and filled the hungry with good
things.

PSALM 17:15

But I will see your face in righteousness;
when I awake, I will be satisfied with
your presence.

MATTHEW 5:43–47

"You have heard that it was said, love your neighbor and hate your enemy. But I tell you, love your enemies and pray for those who persecute you, so that you may be children of your Father in heaven. For he causes his sun to rise on the evil and the good, and sends rain on the righteous and the unrighteous. For if you love those who love you, what reward will you have? Don't even the tax collectors do the same? And if you greet only your brothers and sisters, what are you doing out of the ordinary? Don't even the Gentiles do the same?"

2 CORINTHIANS 13:11

Finally, brothers and sisters, rejoice. Become mature, be encouraged, be of the same mind, be at peace, and the God of love and peace will be with you.

LUKE 14:13–14

"When you host a banquet, invite those who are poor, maimed, lame, or blind. And you will be blessed, because they cannot repay you; for you will be repaid at the resurrection of the righteous."

The Lord is my shepherd;
I have what I need.

He lets me lie down in green pastures;
he leads me beside quiet waters.

He renews my life;
he leads me along the right paths
for his name's sake.

Even when I go through the darkest valley,
I fear no danger,
for you are with me;
your rod and your staff—they comfort me.

You prepare a table before me
in the presence of my enemies;
you anoint my head with oil;
my cup overflows.

Only goodness and faithful love will pursue me
all the days of my life,
and I will dwell in the house of the Lord
as long as I live.

Psalm 23

Chapter 9

Peace in the Oil: Our Balm

Our family loves being outdoors. Starting when the kids were young, we loved going to a local state park with our 8-person tent for a few nights every fall and every spring. But as they got older, for our annual vacation, we started renting a motor home to see different parts of the country. This is more like glamping—glamorous camping—because in a motor home you have a comfy mattress, air conditioner, kitchen, and indoor bathroom. The beauty of the outdoors, but with the comforts of a home on wheels.

On our first motor home adventure, we ventured out west. We saw the immense Grand Canyon, hiked the Narrows of Zion National Park, and walked the rim of Bryce Canyon. The beautiful sites of the western United States are remarkable.

For our second motor home trip, we drove from our home in North Carolina through Pennsylvania and up to Niagara Falls in New York. It was amazing! The sheer volume of water that cascades over those falls is unbelievable. Then, we crossed the Canadian border and spent a few days in a Canadian National Park. As we drove into the campground, it was breathtaking. Beautiful cliffs into clear alpine lakes. Shady, forested camping sites with incredible views.

However, two days after we arrived, terrible mosquitos swarmed in. We were told that the warmer weather of these summer months brought an infestation of these flying pests every year. Anytime we were outside they would swarm us. We tried everything. Bug spray. Insect repellent. Sticky traps. Thermacell zones. Mosquito tents. Nothing worked. They were terrible! And they drove us crazy. Buzzing around our ears. Landing on our arms. Biting us. It was miserable.

I can't help but think of that summer and those swarms of mosquitoes when I learned about the next image in the beautiful poem of Psalm 23. Pesky flies also are a nuisance for sheep, requiring a shepherd to help relieve the sheep with his oil.

A Shepherd's Oil

Before we talk about the oil, I want to show you something really neat about Psalm 23. As we progress through the psalm, David recounts different seasons of a year for a shepherd. It begins with his flock in lower green pastures in the winter. Then he leads them beside quiet waters to other grazing fields in the spring months. They traverse up through mountainous valleys to reach the high tablelands in the summer months. As we discussed in chapter 8, these are fields of fresh tender grass with clear, running springs.

However, just as we learned in Canada, "summertime is fly time . . . hordes of insects emerge with the advent of warm weather."[34] There are several parasites that can swarm a flock in these summer months. Different types of flies, mosquitoes, gnats, and other winged insects are prolific, and their presence can turn the wonderful, warm summer months into times of complete torture for sheep. Their presence, both around their heads and even in their nostrils, will drive the sheep crazy. They become frantic, frustrated, and frenzied. A shepherd's presence with the right tools is essential.

There are three things a shepherd always carries with him. The first two are a rod and a staff, which we discussed in chapters 6 and 7. The oil is the third tool that a shepherd always has with him, which is why David writes in Psalm 23:5: "You anoint my head with oil; my cup overflows." This oil soothed sheep when flies would buzz around their heads in those warm summer months. It prevented parasites and other diseases, and it healed emerging wounds when sheep got various infections.

A shepherd's oil was a simple mixture they could easily make from resources they had all around them. Beginning with olive oil, a shepherd would then add sulfur and some other spices. This mixture gave needed relief to a flock no matter what pest or parasite they were experiencing. There are three different reasons a shepherd would use his oil: to prevent, to soothe, and to heal. These will all be discussed in the sections that follow, and I pray that you will see how a shepherd's oil truly brought peace to his sheep in these warm summer months when flies were swarming.

Preventative Oil

The first reason that a shepherd uses oil is to prevent his sheep from becoming frantic, or even infected, by the unrelenting presence of flies landing on their faces. The moment that sheep experience the swarms of flies, a flock will become anxious and frustrated with the buzzing around (and on) their heads. A healthy sheep holds its head upright and alert, but one who is pestered, sick, or infected, will droop his head down low.[35] Immediately, an attentive shepherd will put the oil on their noses and heads as an antidote and preventative.

This is not a one-time application, however. It needs to be reapplied continually through these summer months. A shepherd smears the oil over the sheep's entire head and around their nose to divert the flies from landing on them. It is a long application process, done individually sheep by sheep, but a shepherd knows that there is no other way to prevent his flock from being driven crazy by the pesky parasites that come with the summer months.

Once the oil is applied, the sheep are no longer aggravated, irritable, and restless. The shepherd's oil refreshes them so that they can graze peacefully and rest comfortably. Perhaps that's why *The Message* paraphrases Psalm 23:5 as "you revive my drooping head." A shepherd's oil prevents and refreshes a sheep from the pesky, annoying flies.

In the same way, the Word of God is like a preventative oil for pesky, annoying thoughts and lies that buzz around our heads. Have you ever had one of those annoying thoughts that drives you crazy? You just can't stop thinking about it, and it affects how you feel, act, and speak. I know I have. Maybe it is an insecurity, a fear, a jealousy, or a hateful thought that just keeps buzzing around your mind no matter what you try to do.

Well, friend, God's Word is like the shepherd's oil for our minds. As we apply the truth of His Word to our minds, it allows His peace to come. We replace the lies with the truth. We substitute the insecurities with the promises of Scripture. We swat away jealousy and hatred, so that we can begin to pray for that person. God's Word is a preventative, repelling oil to these annoying, pesky thoughts. Listen to the beautiful promises of Isaiah 26:3: "You will keep the mind that is dependent on you in perfect peace, for it is trusting in you." We might not be able to keep the fly (or thought) from landing on our heads, but we can prevent it from staying there with the oil of God's Word applied to our minds.

We can echo the truths of the psalmist in Psalm 92:1–4, 10: "It is good to give thanks to the LORD, to sing praise to your name, Most High, to declare your faithful love in the morning and your faithfulness at night, with a ten-stringed harp and the music of a lyre. For you have made me rejoice, LORD, by what you have done; I will shout for joy because of the works of your hands. . . . I have been anointed with the finest oil." When we replace the annoying lies with the truth of God's Word, our minds are anointed with the finest oil, and peace comes.

Soothing Oil

In addition to preventing and repelling the buzzing insects, a shepherd will also apply the oil to soothe the sheep from their worst enemy: the nasal fly. If there is no oil applied there previously, a nasal fly will lay their eggs in the warm mucous at the opening of the sheep's nostril. Then, when the larva hatches, it climbs up into the sheep's nostril and burrows into its nasal cavities. This worm then turns into a fly and begins flying around inside the nostril of the sheep.[36] As you can imagine, the entire process from egg to fly drives a sheep completely crazy.

When a sheep has been infested with nasal flies, it will beat its head on rocks to relieve the irritation inside its head. Sometimes, a sheep will rub its nose completely raw on trees or bushes or even thrash its head around to get relief. In some terrible instances, a sheep will be driven into such a frenzy that it will even go to extreme measures and kill itself to rid itself of the burrowed insect.

A shepherd's oil soothes a sheep with nasal flies. When the oil is applied, the nasal flies cannot lay the eggs there. Even if they did, the eggs and larva are suffocated, bringing instant relief to the sheep. The infesting insects can no longer hatch and burrow. The oil's presence in the sheep's nose, along with the oil's powerful properties, soothes the sheep from this terrible pest and keeps others from multiplying and inhabiting its nostrils too.

For us, burrowing storms can often try to take up residence in our minds and lives, causing us deep distress. God's presence is the divine help we need to soothe us in this frenetic state. I think about the many demon-possessed people that Jesus healed. One of them was driven so crazy by a legion of unclean spirits, that he lived away from the city in the tombs. Mark 5:3–5 describes his distraught state: "No one was able to restrain him anymore—not even with a chain—because he often had been bound with shackles and chains, but had torn the chains apart and smashed the shackles. No one was strong enough to subdue him. Night and day among the tombs and on the mountains, he was always crying out and cutting himself with stones." Can you imagine the absolute agony of this precious man? Yet Jesus saw him and helped him, His presence and power operating like a soothing oil to his mind and body. After Jesus frees him from the demons, the man gets dressed, sits with Jesus, and is in his right mind (v. 15). This man is truly set free and soothed from what plagued him.

Paul promises believers that in Christ Jesus, we are set free too. Listen to Romans 8:1–2, "Therefore, there is now no condemnation for those in Christ Jesus, because the law of the Spirit of life in Christ Jesus has set you free from the law of sin and death." What Christ has done for us on the cross sets us free from the storms caused by sin and death. We no longer need to be tormented by the burrowing, sinful storms that come our way. We can be set free.

There is another occasion where Jesus calmed the storms. Do you recall the story of when the disciples were in the boat and a storm arose out of nowhere on the Sea of Galilee? The disciples were so scared because the waves were crashing onto the boat, and it was beginning to sink. Jesus was asleep, but when they woke Him up, He immediately commanded the wind and the waves to be still. "And there was a great calm" (Matt. 8:26). Just as Jesus calmed the tormented man, He also calmed the storm around the disciples. His presence and power soothes us.

So often we think that our battles are against the things of this world and are fought with the weapons of this world. However, 2 Corinthians 10:4–5 reminds us, "Since the weapons of our warfare are not of the flesh, but are powerful through God for the demolition of strongholds. We demolish arguments and every proud thing that is raised up against the knowledge of God, and we take every thought captive to obey

Christ." To be soothed by Jesus's presence, we need to make sure we are taking every thought captive to Him. When a tormenting thought comes into our minds, we must replace it with the truths of God's presence and promises. Notice what Psalm 107:28–31 reassures us, "Then they cried out to the LORD in their trouble, and he brought them out of their distress. He stilled the storm to a whisper, and the waves of the sea were hushed. They rejoiced when the waves grew quiet. Then he guided them to the harbor they longed for. Let them give thanks to the LORD for his faithful love and his wondrous works for all humanity." The storm was silenced. The waves were hushed. He guided them to a harbor. Talk about the soothing presence of God in our lives.

I'm actually writing this chapter from a hospital room in December 2024. My husband developed a blood clot after a knee injury, and it landed us in the hospital for Christmas this year. This is definitely not how we planned this holiday season or vacation time. However, despite the many medical storms we have faced this week, I have experienced the soothing presence of Immanuel, God with us. Just as we saw in chapter 5, when we walk through the valley, He is with us. And His presence is like a soothing oil to our souls. I can testify to this full well this week. When a fear or tormenting thought would enter my mind, I would replace it with the truth that I have a Good Shepherd who will never leave me or forsake me. And I have felt God's presence, soothing us in this storm.

Healing Oil

In addition to preventing flies and soothing the sheep, a shepherd's oil also heals the sheep. You see, summertime is fly time, but it is also scab time for the sheep. Scab is a highly contagious infection caused by a mite on the sheep's skin. It causes an intense allergic reaction that can spread quickly through a flock by direct contact. A sheep with scab has a number of warning signs: severe itching and scratching, loss of wool, skin infections, weight loss, biting at their sides, and restlessness. Like with the nasal flies, sheep with scab will scratch themselves on fence posts, bite at their fleece, and try to find relief anyway they can from this terrible infection.

In the Old Testament, whenever a verse describes a sheep without blemish, it is referring to a sheep without scab. Over and over in the Levitical law, God commands His people to bring a sheep or a ram without blemish, or in other words, without any scab infections. Listen to the Lord's command for offerings in Leviticus 3:1, "If his offering is a fellowship sacrifice, and he is presenting an animal from the herd, whether male or female, he is to present one *without blemish* before the Lord." What's beautiful is that Hebrews describes Jesus, our Passover Lamb, as being without blemish too:

> But Christ has appeared as a high priest of the good things that have come. In the greater and more perfect tabernacle not made with hands (that is, not of this creation), he entered

> the most holy place once for all time, not by the blood of goats and calves, but by his own blood, having obtained eternal redemption. For if the blood of goats and bulls and the ashes of a young cow, sprinkling those who are defiled, sanctify for the purification of the flesh, how much more will the blood of Christ, who through the eternal Spirit offered himself *without blemish* to God, cleanse our consciences from dead works so that we can serve the living God? (Heb. 9:11–14)

Of course, Jesus didn't have scab, but what this means is that Jesus was free from any contamination or evil. He did not have any parasite or infection. He didn't have a sinful disease that needed to be healed. Nothing impure could burrow into, attach itself to, or take up residence in Him. He was perfect.

Now for sheep, the only antidote for scab is a shepherd's oil. It suffocates the mites, heals the skin irritation, and brings relief from the parasite. However, unlike with the nasal flies, a shepherd has to completely submerge a sheep in the oil to get rid of scab. He will completely dip a sheep in the solution, even submerging the head, to rid the sheep from the pesky mites. The skin, the fleece, the head, the mites, everything needs to be completely submerged in the oil.

In our lives, so often we contaminate our thoughts with the things of this world. We fill our lives with fretful social media, anger-inducing news, ungodly TV episodes, and other worldly ideas that irritate and aggravate. These contaminants, like the scab mites, need to be healed. God's Word reminds us to completely submerge our minds and hearts in prayer, thinking on the praiseworthy things of God. Listen to the instructions of Philippians 4:6–9:

> Don't worry about anything, but in everything, through prayer and petition with thanksgiving, present your requests to God. And the peace of God, which surpasses all understanding, will guard your hearts and minds in Christ Jesus. Finally brothers and sisters, whatever is true, whatever is honorable, whatever is just, whatever is pure, whatever is lovely, whatever is commendable—if there is any moral excellence and if there is anything praiseworthy—dwell on these things. Do what you have learned and received and heard from me, and seen in me, and the God of peace will be with you.

If we allow the contagious, infectious ideals of this world to take root in our lives, we will be miserable. However, if we submerge our thoughts and minds in prayer to God, His healing and soothing peace will follow. This is why David can say, "My cup overflows." *The Message* paraphrases Psalm 23:5 as "my cup brims with blessing" and *The Living Bible* says,

"Blessings overflow!" In other words, we can have lives of overflowing peace and blessing when we submerge ourselves in God's Word and His presence. He is our healer. Relish the words of Psalm 147:3–6: "He heals the brokenhearted and bandages their wounds. He counts the number of the stars; he gives names to all of them. Our Lord is great, vast in power; his understanding is infinite. The LORD helps the oppressed but brings the wicked to the ground." The Lord is our Healer—or as the Hebrew would render it, *Jehovah Rapha*.

The Holy Spirit Is Our Balm

Just like a shepherd's oil prevents, soothes, and heals a sheep, our God is our soothing oil and balm too. As we looked at in this chapter, His Word brings peace to our minds. It is with the truths and promises of Scripture that the pesky and annoying thoughts and lies are repelled and soothed.

But among the 200 times that oil is mentioned in the Bible, it is most closely connected with the Holy Spirit's presence and actions.[37] In the Old Testament, if a person was anointed with oil it represented that they were put into a position of authority and ultimately set apart for a specific purpose. In other words, kings, prophets, or priests would be anointed with the Holy Spirit, empowering them to be a person used by God. For example, Exodus 28:41 describes Aaron being anointed as priest. In 1 Samuel 16:13, the prophet Samuel anoints David as the next king of Israel: "So Samuel took the horn of oil and anointed him in the presence of his brothers, and the Spirit of the LORD came powerfully on David from that day forward." And in 1 Kings 19:16, God anointed Elisha as a prophet.

Old Testament prophecies also connect oil with the term "Messiah." This Hebrew word can also be translated as "The Anointed One." Jesus Christ, as the promised Messiah, was anointed with the Holy Spirit to do God's work. Look at these words in Acts 10:38: "God anointed Jesus of Nazareth with the Holy Spirit and with power, and how he went about doing good and healing all who were under the tyranny of the devil, because God was with him." He is the Anointed One and says, "The Spirit of the Lord is on me, because he has anointed me to preach good news to the poor. He has sent me to proclaim release to the captives and recovery of sight to the blind, to set free the oppressed" (Luke 4:18).

And then, the New Testament describes God's Spirit as being poured out on us. Just like the anointing oil was poured onto the head of those that were appointed, the Holy Spirit is poured out, blessing and anointing us. The apostle John tells the early church: "But you have an anointing from the Holy One, and all of you know the truth. . . . As for you, the anointing you received from him remains in you, and you don't need anyone to teach you. Instead, his anointing teaches you about all things" (1 John 2:20, 27). The Holy Spirit is the one who reminds and teaches us about God. We can understand the truths of God because the Holy Spirit has anointed our hearts and minds. This is why Jesus says it is better for Him to go back to heaven so that the Father will send the Holy Spirit to us: "But the Counselor, the Holy Spirit, whom the Father will send in my name, will teach you all things and remind you of everything I have told you" (John 14:26). I'm so thankful for the Counselor, our Holy Spirit, who has anointed us with His understanding. He is a deposit for our inheritance in God's kingdom and the one who seals us as belonging to Him: "Now it is God who . . . has anointed us. He has also put his seal on us and given us the Spirit in our hearts as a down payment" (2 Cor. 1:21–22). Friend, what good news! The Holy Spirit truly is the means by which our lives are anointed with His peace.

I love the promises of 1 Peter 5:10 (NIV): "And the God of all grace, who called you to his eternal glory in Christ, after you have suffered a little while, will himself restore you and make you strong, firm and steadfast." Our Good Shepherd is our soothing and healing balm. He Himself is the oil that prevents, heals, and calms. Just like sheep would be anointed with oil, we are anointed with the Holy Spirit. It is only in Him we can experience lives of overflowing peace.

Questions to Consider

1. Have you ever experienced an annoying swarm of insects or pests? What emotions did it cause for you? Can you relate to how the sheep feel?

2. When an annoying thought or pesky lie comes to your mind, how do you fight it with the truth of God's Word? How is God's Word like an oil to your mind?

3. Why did God command that His people bring a sheep without scab to be offered to Him? How does this truth make Jesus, the Lamb without blemish, even more precious to us?

4. What storms have come into your life? Have you ever experienced the soothing presence of the Holy Spirit in those storms?

5. How can you submerge your heart and your mind in God's Word? What habits need to be changed so that you are dipped in truth, rather than the contaminants of this world?

Verses for Reflection

PSALM 45:7

You love righteousness and hate
   wickedness;
therefore God, your God, has anointed
   you with the oil of joy.

LAMENTATIONS 3:22–24

"Because of the LORD's faithful love
we do not perish,
for his mercies never end.
They are new every morning;
great is your faithfulness!
I say, "The LORD is my portion,
therefore I will put my hope in him."

MATTHEW 11:28–30

"Come to me, all of you who are weary and burdened, and I will give you rest. Take my yoke upon you and learn from me, because I am lowly and humble in heart, and you will find rest for your souls. For my yoke is easy and my burden is light."

ROMANS 12:2

Do not be conformed to this age, but be transformed by the renewing of your mind, so that you may discern what is the good, pleasing, and perfect will of God.

GALATIANS 5:16–25

Walk by the Spirit and you will certainly not carry out the desire of the flesh. For the flesh desires what is against the Spirit, and the Spirit desires what is against the flesh; these are opposed to each other, so that you don't do what you want. But if you are led by the Spirit, you are not under the law. Now the works of the flesh are obvious: sexual immorality, moral impurity, promiscuity, idolatry, sorcery, hatreds, strife, jealousy, outbursts of anger, selfish ambitions, dissensions, factions, envy, drunkenness, carousing, and anything similar. I am warning you about these things—as I warned you before—that those who practice such things will not inherit the kingdom of God. But the fruit of the Spirit is love, joy, peace, patience, kindness, goodness, faithfulness, gentleness, and self-control. The law is not against such things. Now those who belong to Christ Jesus have crucified the flesh with its passions and desires. If we live by the Spirit, let us also keep in step with the Spirit.

The Lord is my shepherd;
I have what I need.

He lets me lie down in green pastures;
he leads me beside quiet waters.

He renews my life;
he leads me along the right paths
for his name's sake.

Even when I go through the darkest valley,
I fear no danger,
for you are with me;
your rod and your staff—they comfort me.

You prepare a table before me
in the presence of my enemies;
you anoint my head with oil;
my cup overflows.

Only goodness and faithful love
will pursue me
all the days of my life,
and I will dwell in the house of the Lord
as long as I live.

Psalm 23

Chapter 10

Peace in the House of the Lord: Our Dwelling

Home.

When you read this word, what comes to mind? Maybe you think about your childhood home, with your old bedroom and the comforts of your elementary years. Maybe you picture your parents' home, and the smell of chocolate chip cookies and a warm guest bed waiting for you when you come visit. Maybe you imagine your own home with the comforts of your own squishy sofa and soft blankets. Maybe you think of the mountains or the beach, where extended family lives and you gather for reunions.

Friend, there is one place that is our most real home, yet I can imagine it is not what you pictured. I bet none of us thought of heaven! More than your mom's house, or the cabin on your family's land, or your residence now, the new heavens and the new earth is our real home (Revelation 21). Philippians 3:20 reminds us that this world is not our home, but rather "our citizenship is in heaven."

The author of Hebrews writes about so many heroes of our faith that were "longing for a better country—a heavenly one" (Heb. 11:16 NIV). They knew that this world was not our home. Listen to David's prayer: "For we are *strangers* before you and *sojourners*, as all our fathers were. Our days on the earth are like a shadow, and there is no abiding" (1 Chron. 29:15 ESV). Consider Hebrews 11:9–10 about Abraham: "By faith he stayed as a *foreigner* in the land of promise, living in tents as did Isaac and Jacob, coheirs of the same promise. For he was looking forward to the city that has foundations, whose architect and builder is God." Read the words of Peter: "Dear friends, I urge you as *strangers* and *exiles* to abstain from sinful desires that wage war against the soul" (1 Pet. 2:11). Did you notice all those italicized words? These biblical heroes knew that they were merely foreigners, strangers, exiles, and sojourners here on earth. Just passing through. Their real home was heaven.

I read a quote from Randy Alcorn a few weeks ago that resonated with me so deeply: "Nothing is more often misdiagnosed than our homesickness for heaven. We think that what we want is sex, drugs, alcohol, a new job, a raise, a doctorate, a spouse, a large screen television, a new car, a cabin in the woods, a condo in Hawaii. What we really want is the person we were made for, Jesus, and the place we were made for, Heaven. Nothing less can satisfy us."[38] We were made for a different place, a place where we will dwell with our God forever.

Ecclesiastes 3:11 explains that God has "put eternity in their hearts." We don't really have an English word that encapsulates this concept, but the German language does: *sehnsucht*. It is an inconsolable longing in the human heart for something we don't know—a yearning for a far, familiar, non-earthly land that one can identify as one's home. If you've ever read any of C. S. Lewis's works, you know how he describes this longing:

> The books or the music in which we thought the beauty was located will betray us if we trust to them; it was not in them, it only came through them, and what came through them was longing. These things—the beauty, the memory of our own past—are good images of what we really desire; but if they are mistaken for the thing itself they turn into dumb idols, breaking the hearts of their worshippers. For they are not the thing itself; they are only the scent of a flower we have not found, the echo of a tune we have not heard, news from a country we have never visited. . . . Do you

> think I am trying to weave a spell? Perhaps I am; but remember your fairy tales. Spells are used for breaking enchantments as well as for inducing them. And you and I have need of the strongest spell that can be found to wake us up from the evil enchantment of worldliness which has been laid upon us for nearly a hundred years. Almost our whole education has been directing to silencing this shy, persistent, inner voice; almost all our modern philosophies have been devised to convince us that the good of man is to be found on this earth.[39]

What we were made for is not found on this fallen earth. We long for a heavenly home. So remember, my friend, we are just sojourners now, traveling through until one day it will be "on earth as it is in heaven" (Matt. 6:10).

A Wake of Goodness and Love

Psalm 23 ends with the most beautiful verse and promise of peace: We will get to dwell with our God forever. Friend, though verse 6 is familiar, I pray you can see it with new eyes: "Only goodness and faithful love will pursue me all the days of my life, and I will dwell in the house of the LORD as long as I live."

Let's savor every word of this last verse, so that we can truly understand what it means to have a life of overflowing peace in our Good Shepherd.

"Only . . ." The Christian Standard Bible begins this verse with the word "only." It means "solely or exclusively." Other translations say "surely" (NIV, ESV), which means "with certainty." That means that we can say with confidence and assurance that nothing bad will ever come from your Good Shepherd. James 1:17 reminds us, "Every good and perfect gift is from above, coming down from the Father of lights, who does not change like shifting shadows." He is a Good Shepherd, and only goodness and faithful kindness come from Him.

". . . Goodness and faithful love . . ." Let's look at these two words that the Bible promises will come from Him: goodness and faithful love. The NKJV says "goodness and mercy," whereas *The Living Bible* says "unfailing kindness." These are all the same concepts. It is the overflowing generous bounty by which He extends blessings to His creation. When we experience God's goodness we enjoy benevolence, generosity, sweetness, and kindness, because His goodness is the broad category which encompasses several of His moral attributes. For example, His goodness toward those in pain we call *mercy*. His goodness toward those deserving judgment we call *patience*. His goodness toward those who are guilty we call *grace*. His goodness toward those who are undeserving we call *love*. Friend, never take it for granted: your well-being, your wholeness, your shalom peace comes straight from the heart of your Good Shepherd. Everything we receive flows from Him and out of His goodness.

". . . will pursue me all the days of my life . . ." Not only does this wonderful goodness of God flow to us, but it will also pursue us for the rest of our life. This concept of pursuit can be worded as "follow" (NIV) or "chase" (*The Message*). This is another agricultural concept that I didn't know about sheep. They are called the animals with "golden hooves," because they leave behind well-fertilized and weed-free pastures. Sheep are a benefit to the land. Behind them flows blessings.

So, what do you leave behind you? What comes from your legacy? Just as a boat leaves a wake behind it, so does your life. Make sure you are leaving a wake of goodness and faithful love. Galatians 6:7 reminds us that "God is not mocked. For whatever a person sows he will also reap." Are you sowing seeds of peace or turmoil, love or hate, forgiveness or bitterness? May what comes after us be a blessing for those who follow.

". . . and I will dwell in the house of the Lord as long as I live." What a beautiful promise! Don't just gloss over this statement like a platitude or a meme. This is not a social media quote or a bumper sticker. It is a sure guarantee. Look at the verb tense: I WILL dwell. *The Living Bible* paraphrases verse 6 as "I will live with you forever in your home" and *The Message* says, "I'm back home in the house of GOD for the rest of my life." Back home. If you are a Christian, then you will be welcomed into your Father's house that He is preparing for you: "Don't let your heart be troubled. Believe in God; believe also in me. In my Father's house are many rooms. If it were not so, would I have told you that I am going to prepare a place for you? If I go away and prepare a place for you, I will come again and take you to myself, so that where I am you may be also" (John 14:1–3). Your God is preparing a home for you to live with Him.

Did you know that there is another way that Psalm 23:5 could be interpreted that flows right along with this thought? Oil was always kept at the door of a house to welcome guests. After a long day of travel on the dirty, dusty roads, a weary traveler was welcomed with a sweet oil or perfume that refreshed them (Luke 7:46). Being anointed with oil or perfume was a sign of blessing. Jesus is waiting for you, sojourner, with open arms, to welcome you home and anoint your head with oil. Indeed, my friend, blessings will overflow.

God Desires to Dwell with His People

Before we conclude this chapter, I want to show you how God has always desired to dwell with His people. He wants for us to be at home with Him. In John 15:4, Jesus makes this desire so clear: "Remain in Me, and I [will remain] in you" (AMP). It can also be paraphrased, "Live in Me. Make your home in me just as I do in you" (MSG). Let's trace this theme of dwelling from Genesis to Revelation so you can see the beautiful heart of God who loves His people and desires to dwell with them. I pray it increases our desire for our heavenly home!

First, consider the garden of Eden in Genesis 1–3. God dwelled with Adam and Eve there and we are told He walked in the garden with them (Gen. 3:8). God didn't create humans because He was lonely or because He needed anything. He created us out of the love that already existed in the unity of the triune God. After sin entered the world, God clothed them with animal skins (v. 21) and then protected them from reaching the Tree of Life and staying in that fallen, sinful state forever. By casting them out of the garden, He displayed His faithful love and mercy (vv. 22–24).

But God desired to still dwell with His people, and covenanted with Abraham, Isaac, and Jacob (Gen. 12:1–3) to bless all nations. After several generations, God appeared to Moses (Exodus 3) and once again called out His people to live with Him. On the way to the Promised Land, He led them through the wilderness as a pillar of cloud by day and a pillar of fire by night (Exod. 13:21). Since His people were nomads in tents, He too wanted to dwell with His people in a tent. He said, "*I will dwell among the Israelites* and be their God. And they will know that I am the Lord their God, who brought them out of the land of Egypt, *so that I might dwell among them.* I am the Lord their God" (Exod. 29:45–46). His "tently dwelling" was called the tabernacle, described in Exodus 25:8–9: "They are to make a sanctuary for me *so that I may dwell among them.* You must make it according to all that I show you—the pattern of the tabernacle as well as the pattern of all its furnishings." (And I don't have enough time or space to describe it, but you will find references to the tabernacle in the heavenly descriptions of Revelation! The tabernacle truly was a foreshadowing of what is to come when we will dwell with our God in heaven.)

Once His people entered the Promised Land, God continued to set His people apart as His own nation. He fought battles for them and instituted laws to keep them pure and safe. Over and over, He reiterated His desire to dwell with them: "If you follow my statutes and faithfully observe my commands, . . . *I will place my residence among you*, and I will not reject you. I will walk among you and be your God, and you will be my people. I am the LORD your God, who brought you out of the land of Egypt, so that you would no longer be their slaves. I broke the bars of your yoke and enabled you to live in freedom" (Lev. 26:3, 11–13).

Finally, God established His permanent dwelling place in Jerusalem with King David. However, it bothered David that he lived in a palace while God still dwelled in a tent. Listen to God's response in 2 Samuel 7:5–7, 11–13:

> "Are you to build me a house to dwell in? From the time I brought the Israelites out of Egypt until today I have not dwelt in a house; instead, I have been moving around

> with a tent as my dwelling. In all my journeys with all the Israelites, have I ever spoken a word to one of the tribal leaders of Israel, whom I commanded to shepherd my people Israel, asking: Why haven't you built me a house of cedar?' . . . The LORD declares to you: The LORD himself will make a house for you. When your time comes and you rest with your ancestors, I will raise up after you your descendant, who will come from your body, and I will establish his kingdom. He is the one who will build a house for my name, and I will establish the throne of his kingdom forever."

So King David's son, Solomon, builds a permanent dwelling for the Lord. It is the temple, built on Mount Zion in Jerusalem. As soon as Solomon prays and dedicates the temple, God's presence consumed it:

> Fire descended from heaven and consumed the burnt offering and the sacrifices, and the glory of the LORD filled the temple. The priests were not able to enter the LORD's temple because the glory of the LORD filled the temple of the LORD. All the Israelites were watching when the fire descended and the glory of the LORD came on the temple. They

> bowed down on the pavement with their faces to the ground. They worshiped and praised the LORD: For he is good, for his faithful love endures forever. (2 Chron. 7:1–4)

Sadly, the Israelites disobeyed God's commands, and their kingdom was divided. Even the temple was destroyed, but God continued to make His desire to dwell with His people evident through the prophets. Read His promise through the prophet Ezekiel:

> "I will make a covenant of peace with them; it will be a permanent covenant with them. I will establish and multiply them and will set my sanctuary among them forever. *My dwelling place will be with them;* I will be their God, and they will be my people. When my sanctuary is among them forever, the nations will know that I, the LORD, sanctify Israel." (Ezek. 37:26–28)

Other nations began capturing the Israelites and exiling them to different nations. While in Persia, the prophet Nehemiah remembers God's promises and prays: "Please remember what you commanded your servant Moses: 'If you are unfaithful, I will scatter you among the peoples. But if you return to me and carefully observe my commands, even though your exiles were banished to the farthest horizon, I will gather them from there and bring them to the place *where I chose to have my name dwell*'" (Neh. 1:8–9). It is the prophet Nehemiah that God uses to rebuild Jerusalem. God speaks a similar reminder through the prophet Zechariah:

> "Daughter Zion, shout for joy and be glad, for *I am coming to dwell among you*"—this is the LORD's declaration. "Many nations will join themselves to the LORD on that day and become my people. *I will dwell among you,* and you will know that the LORD of Armies has sent me to you." (Zech. 2:10–11)

Most important, after 400 years, God keeps His promise and comes to dwell with His people again, but this time, it is in a form they had never experienced before. He no longer dwelled in a tently tabernacle, or a pillar of cloud or fire consuming the temple. He came in bodily form—His name is Jesus! John 1:1–18 describes this amazing incarnation (God embodied in the flesh). I think verses 1–2 and 14 are especially beautiful in light of this theme of dwelling that we have been tracing since Genesis: "In the beginning was the Word, and the Word was with God, and the Word was God. He was with God in the beginning. . . . *The Word became flesh and dwelt among us.* We observed his glory, the glory as the one and only Son from the Father, full of grace and truth." God Himself took on humanity (Phil. 2:6–8) so that He could once again dwell with His people and make a way for them to dwell with

Him forever in heaven (John 14:6). He promised to return one day to bring us there. Until then, He is preparing a room for us in heaven so that we can dwell with Him: "In my Father's house are many rooms. If it were not so, would I have told you that I am going to prepare a place for you? If I go away and prepare a place for you, I will come again and take you to myself, so that where I am you may be also" (John 14:2–3).

Today, those of us who are Christians experience the dwelling of God through His Holy Spirit. The apostle Paul reminds us of this beautiful truth often in his letters: "Don't you yourselves know that you are God's temple and that the Spirit of God lives in you? If anyone destroys God's temple, God will destroy him; for God's temple is holy, and that is what you are" (1 Cor. 3:16–17). In Ephesians 2:19–22, he reminds us of the beautiful household of God that is the Church: "So, then, you are no longer foreigners and strangers, but fellow citizens with the saints, and members of God's household, built on the foundation of the apostles and prophets, with Christ Jesus himself as the cornerstone. In him the whole building, being put together, grows into a holy temple in the Lord. In him you are also being built together for *God's dwelling* in the Spirit."

One day, Jesus will return, and we will dwell in the new heavens and new earth with our God forever (Rev. 21:1–5). There will be no more night, no more crying, pain, or tears. His goodness and love and peace will be ours forever. This is our real home and the one we are longing for:

> Then I heard a loud voice from the throne: Look, *God's dwelling is with humanity, and he will live with them.* They will be his peoples, and God himself will be with them and will be their God. He will wipe away every tear from their eyes. Death will be no more; grief, crying, and pain will be no more, because the previous things have passed away. Then the one seated on the throne said, "Look, I am making everything new." He also said, "Write, because these words are faithful and true." Then he said to me, "It is done! I am the Alpha and the Omega, the beginning and the end. I will freely give to the thirsty from the spring of the water of life. The one who conquers will inherit these things, and I will be his God, and he will be my son." (Rev. 21:3–7)

I love how Ezekiel 48:35 describes the heavenly city:

> "The name of the city from that day on will be The Lord Is There."

Home. It is where God is.

Peace in the House of the Lord

Psalm 23:6 (NIV) concludes with this beautiful promise, "And I will dwell in the house of the Lord forever." Friend, that is peace. It is what we were made for: to dwell with our God. A life of wholeness, goodness, beauty, and shalom is not found in the things of this fallen earth. It is found in dwelling with our God in the new heavens and the new earth. That is why David sang, "Better a day in your courts than a thousand anywhere else. I would rather stand at the threshold of the house of my God than live in the tents of wicked people" (Ps. 84:10).

So until we reach heaven, may we make our hearts at home with Him. We do this by loving our Savior and keeping His commands. Listen to Jesus's words in John 14:23: "If anyone loves me, he will keep my word. My Father will love him, and we will come to him and make our home with him." This is truly the secret to a life of overflowing peace.

Jesus: Our Good Shepherd

It is hard to believe that we have come to the end of this beautiful psalm. It is so rich in imagery and lessons for our life. Through these ten chapters, I hope you have seen how we really are like sheep. We are clumsy, dirty, and can get ourselves in some real trouble. And oh how we need a Shepherd, who can lead us, guide us, and be with us through the seasons of life!

Friend, I must tell you one last story about sheep before we end. In December 2015, Jamie and I were gifted a trip to the Holy Land. To this day, it is one of my favorite trips of my entire life. To walk where Jesus walked. To visit the places He came to redeem. To see the Bible come alive. On one of our last days, I had an encounter with sheep and a shepherd that I will never forget. We were walking on the Temple Mount and had just come down the Triumphal Entry road, where Jesus would have ridden the donkey over the spread palm branches while the people cheered, "*Hosanna!*" (John 12:13).

As I am taking in the sights around me, I hear the bleating of sheep coming onto the Temple Mount. My heart was filled with excitement because I have always loved sheep! I saw a shepherd with his staff leading two sheep through the Sheep Gate and along the narrow cobblestone street. I was mesmerized because he was an actual, authentic shepherd, with large, wooly sheep, in the Holy Land of Israel! Psalm 23 was becoming real right before my eyes! Suddenly, the shepherd opens the trunk of a small, 1990's Toyota Corolla. Well, I sure wasn't expecting that! Then, he proceeds to pick up the first sheep and load it into the trunk of the car! Yes, you heard me right. The sheep is bleating loudly and protesting because he will not fit. Then, the shepherd picks up a second sheep and smooshes him into the trunk too. I was dumbfounded! What on earth? Slamming the trunk shut, with the two sheep bleating inside, the shepherd gets into the car and just drives away. I stood there completely speechless and paralyzed. I couldn't believe what I just witnessed. Just then, our sweet Israeli tour guide came over to me and said, "That was not a good shepherd. Our Shepherd is Jesus and He is good."

I have never forgotten that truth. Yes, yes He is.

What a beautiful Shepherd we have! He is our Provider. He is our Living Water and our Daily Bread. He is our Righteousness and Freedom. He is our Protector and Healer. He is our Immanuel, our Comforter, and our Salve. He is our Satisfaction and our Dwelling Place. He is our Good Shepherd, and we as His sheep are loved and taken care of.

Do you want to know the secret to a life of overflowing peace? Look no further than Jesus. He is your Good Shepherd and in Him you have everything you need. As you read these words one last time, let all that you have learned about your Good Shepherd reverberate in your heart and mind:

The Lord is my Shepherd [to feed,
to guide and to shield me],
I shall not want.

He lets me lie down in green pastures;
He leads me beside the still and quiet waters.

He refreshes and restores my soul (life);
He leads me in the paths of righteousness
for His name's sake.

Even though I walk through the [sunless] valley
of the shadow of death,
I fear no evil, for You are with me;
Your rod [to protect] and Your staff [to guide],
they comfort and console me.

You prepare a table before me in the presence of
my enemies.
You have anointed and refreshed
my head with oil;
My cup overflows.

Surely goodness and mercy and unfailing love
shall follow me all the days of my life,
And I shall dwell forever [throughout all my days]
in the house and in the presence of the LORD.

Psalm 23 (AMP)

Questions to Consider

1. What images came to your mind when you heard the word *home*?

2. Have you ever experienced a "heavenly homesickness" like Randy Alcorn or C. S. Lewis described?

3. What kind of "wake" are you leaving? What follows after you in your legacy right now?

4. Of all the images of God dwelling with His people from Genesis to Revelation, which one was new to you?

Which one had you heard before? Which one do you want to meditate on more?

5. A life of peace is found in our Good Shepherd. Which name of God resonates with you the most today: Provider? Living Water? Daily Bread? Righteousness? Freedom? Protector? Healer? Immanuel? Comforter? Salve? Satisfaction? Dwelling Place? Jesus? Close in prayer thanking Jesus for being these for you. You have everything you need.

Verses for Reflection

ISAIAH 57:15

For the High and Exalted One,
who lives forever, whose name is holy,
says this:
"I live in a high and holy place,
and with the oppressed and lowly of
spirit,
to revive the spirit of the lowly
and revive the heart of the oppressed."

PSALM 65:4

How happy is the one you choose
and bring near to live in your courts!
We will be satisfied with the goodness
of your house,
the holiness of your temple.

PSALM 140:13

Surely the righteous will praise your
name;
the upright will live in your presence.

EPHESIANS 3:16–19

I pray that he may grant you, according to the riches of his glory, to be strengthened with power in your inner being through his Spirit, and that Christ may dwell in your hearts through faith. I pray that you, being rooted and firmly established in love, may be able to comprehend with all the saints what is the length and width, height and depth of God's love, and to know Christ's love that surpasses knowledge, so that you may be filled with all the fullness of God.

Appendix

Have You Met Jesus, the Good Shepherd?

I am so thankful that you have turned to this page. Your Good Shepherd loves you and wants to rescue you! He wants to have a personal relationship with you, knowing and calling you by name.

But in order to start that relationship, there are a few things you must talk to God about in prayer:

Confess to God that you are a sinner.

- Romans 3:23 says, "For all have sinned and fall short of the glory of God."
- Sin is anything that we love more than God. These might be specific sins or just general sins of not seeking and obeying Him. Tell God what sins you have committed.

Repent of your sin.

- Luke 13:3 reminds us, "No . . . unless you repent, you will all perish."
- Romans 6:23, "For the wages of sin is death, but the gift of God is eternal life in Christ Jesus our Lord."
- Our sin deserves death. But when we repent, it means we are willing to stop sinning. Tell God that you want to turn away from your sins with His help.

Ask God to cleanse and forgive you through the blood of Jesus Christ, shed on the cross.

- First John 1:9 says, "If we confess our sins, he is faithful and righteous to forgive us our sins and to cleanse us from all unrighteousness."
- Jesus paid the price for our sin by dying on the cross for you and for me. Believe that He died for you, was buried, and was raised on the third day, according to the Scriptures (1 Cor. 15:3–4). And it is only by His blood that you are cleansed and forgiven.

Invite Jesus to come into your life, taking control as Lord and Shepherd.

- Romans 10:9 promises, "If you confess with your mouth, 'Jesus is Lord,' and believe in your heart that God raised him from the dead, you will be saved."
- Ephesians 2:8–9 goes on, "For you are saved by grace through faith, and this is not from yourselves; it is God's gift—not from works, so that no one can boast."
- Thank God for the gift of Jesus and invite Him to lead, guide, and direct you from now on.

Believe God's Word that you are saved!

- John 1:12 proclaims, "But to all who did receive him, he gave them the right to be children of God, to those who believe in his name."
- You are now "born again" (John 3:3) and have established a personal relationship with Him through faith in Christ Jesus! Welcome to His family (and flock)!

Acknowledgments

I am abundantly grateful for my Shepherd, who saved me, called me, and has given me a passion to teach His Word. Before a single word of *Overflowing Peace* was written down in a manuscript, the concepts and lessons found in Psalm 23 were shared with ladies in retreats, Bible studies, and conferences around the country. I love women and I love God's Word. The privilege of serving both is not lost on me. Writing for me is a newer path, but I am so thankful for this life of following Jesus, who has led me down these new paths for His name's sake. He is my Immanuel, and I am so thankful.

To my family, thank you for encouraging me and praying for me in writing this second book. Jamie, I will never forget the night you looked at me and said, "I think it's time for you to write another book." You have always believed in me and challenged me to press on. Thank you for reading my words and thoughts before anyone else. I'm so thankful for your edits, guidance, and help. I love you. Natalie, Nathan, Samuel, and Samantha, you have been my cheerleaders every step of the way! I love being your mom. I will never forget us laughing together on the couch as we watched sheep videos. Researching with you is just way more fun! I think you always pick the best book covers too.

To my friends who have prayed for me in this writing process, thank you. I have cherished and needed them so desperately! Your texts and emails "just checking in" encouraged me so much in some of the hardest and longest writing days. Special thanks to my friends who read the manuscript and gave me such helpful feedback (Rebekah Callahan, Bethany Cooper, Josie Davison, Brianna Oakley, Shann Phillips, and Rachel Reeves) as well as my mom (Linda Baker) and my girls (Natalie and Samantha Dew).

I'm also so thankful for the incredible team at B&H Publishing, particularly my editor Ashley Gorman. Her encouragement has motivated me, and her sharp theological mind and keen eye have made this book sound and relatable. I truly love working with you, Ashley!

To the New Orleans Baptist Theological Seminary and Leavell College family, it is a privilege to belong to you. I love seeing what God is doing in and through you! I love serving alongside our faculty and staff, as well as the Prepare Her Team. The way you are using your gifts and talents for His kingdom spurs me on. I pray this book is a blessing to you too!

And finally, to every woman who picks up and reads this book: Thank you! May you truly come to know the Good Shepherd who loves you so much. It is my prayer that "the peace of God, which surpasses all understanding, will guard your hearts and minds in Christ Jesus" (Phil. 4:7). It is a privilege to serve you.

Notes

1. Much of the cultural information about sheep and shepherds was learned from W. Phillip Keller's book, *A Shepherd Looks at Psalm 23: Discovering God's Love for You* (Zondervan, 2007).

2. https://www.blueletterbible.org/study/misc/name_god.cfm

3. Dr. Angel Martinez, "The Lord Is My Shepherd, 23rd Psalm" (sermon), South Heights Baptist Church, February 9, 1986, https://www.southheightsbaptist.com/play.php.

4. Jen Wilkin, *In His Image: 10 Ways God Calls Us to Reflect His Character* (Crossway, 2018), 47.

5. "At the Glorious Cross," by Daniel Renstrom and Kayla Norton (Brooks Hill Worship, 2023), https://www.multitracks.com/songs/Brook-Hills-Worship/Judah's-Lion/At-The-Glorious-Cross/.

6. Adrian Rogers, *The Lord Is My Shepherd: Reflections on God's Loving Care* (Crossway Books, 1999), 18.

7. "He Lives," by A. H. Ackley, 1933 (copyright renewed in 1961, Word Music, Inc).

8. John N. Oswalt and Allen P. Ross, *Genesis & Exodus*, Cornerstone Biblical Commentary (Tyndale House, 2008).

9. Chip Hutcheson, "'Lostness' continues to be world's greatest problem, Chitwood says," *Kentucky Today*, November 16, 2022, https://www.kentuckytoday.com/baptist_life/lostness-continues-to-be-worlds-greatest-problem-chitwood-says/article_21bd5bcc-6536-11ed-8b29-cb66c011f6b5.html.

10. Keller, *A Shepherd Looks at Psalm 23*, 41–42.

11. Keller, *A Shepherd Looks at Psalm 23*, 42.

12. "Jesus' Seven 'I Am' Statements," Thomas Nelson Bibles, November 9, 2018, https://www.thomasnelsonbibles.com/blog/jesus-seven-i-am-statements/.

13. Trevin Wax, "How Is Jesus the Living Bread?" The Gospel Coalition, January 22, 2007, https://www.thegospelcoalition.org/blogs/trevin-wax/how-is-jesus-the-living-bread/.

14. "Savior, Like a Shepherd Lead Us," by Dorothy A. Thrupp, 1836.

15. "Parasympathetic Nervous System (PSNS)," Cleveland Clinic, https://my.clevelandclinic.org/health/body/23266-parasympathetic-nervous-system-psns.

16. *The Hunger Games*, directed by Gary Ross (Santa Monica, CA: Lionsgate, 2012).

17. Water Science School, "The Water in You: Water and the Human Body," USGS, May 22, 2019, https://www.usgs.gov/special-topics/water-science-school/science/water-you-water-and-human-body.

18. Keller, *A Shepherd Looks at Psalm 23*, 58.

19. Signe G. Balch, "Nutrition of Sheep," Merck Veterinary Manual, September 2024, https://www.merckvetmanual.com/management-and-nutrition/preventative-health-care-and-husbandry-of-sheep/nutrition-of-sheep.

20. *Baker Encyclopedia of the Bible, Vol. 1 & 2*, ed. Walter A. Elwell (Baker, 1988), 622.

21. Martin Manset, *Dictionary of Bible Themes* (2009), Logos, article 4814 Dew.

22. Sevil Omer, "Global water crisis: Facts, FAQs, and how to help," *World Vision*, March 6, 2025, https://www.worldvision.org/clean-water-news-stories/global-water-crisis-facts#facts.

23. "More children killed by unsafe water, than bullets, says UNICEF chief, UN News, March 21, 2019, https://news.un.org/en/story/2019/03/1035171.

24. Keller, *A Shepherd Looks at Psalm 23*, 84.

25. "Trust and Obey," by John H. Sammis, 1887. Public domain.

26. "Nyctophobia, (Fear of the Dark)," Cleveland Clinic, https://my.clevelandclinic.org/health/diseases/22785-nyctophobia-fear-of-the-dark.

27. "Violent crime time of day (per 1,000 in age group)," OJJDP, https://ojjdp.ojp.gov/statistical-briefing-book/offending-by-youth/faqs/qa03401.

28. "Time of Day and Demographic Perspective of Fatal Alchohol-Impaired-Driving Crashes," U.S. Department of Transportation, August 2011, https://crashstats.nhtsa.dot.gov/Api/Public/ViewPublication/811523.

29. Marc Turnage, "Biblical Israel: Wadi Qilt," CBN Israel, August 31, 2021, https://cbnisrael.org/2021/08/31/biblical-israel-wadi-qilt/#:~:text=Over%20the%20course%20of%20these,850%20feet%20below%20sea%20level.

30. https://www.christianforums.com/threads/did-shepherds-really-break-a-lambs-leg-on-purpose.3295088/

31. Rogers, *The Lord Is My Shepherd*, 49.

32. J. R. R. Tolkien's poem "The Riddle of Strider" in *The Fellowship of the Ring* (HarperCollins, 2012), 170.

33. "Amazing Grace," by John Newton, 1779. Public domain.

34. Keller, *A Shepherd Looks at Psalm 23*, 138.

35. "How Do I Know If I Have Healthy Sheep?" Bar-Bar-A, https://www.horsedrinker.com/telling-if-you-have-healthy-sheep/?srsltid=AfmBOoqvW3pQjOQ8IfwSj1wacZuB8yMhMC44-OxJ3OdKdWK4AIDQuJL6.

36. "Sheep Nasal Bot Myiasis," Merck Veterinary Manual, Updated September 2024, https://www.merckvetmanual.com/respiratory-system/respiratory-diseases-of-sheep-and-goats/sheep-nasal-bot-myiasis.

37. "Oil," *Evangelical Dictionary of Biblical Theology*, ed. Walter A. Elwell, 2nd ed. (Baker, 2001).

38. Randy Alcorn, *Heaven* (Eternal Perspectives Ministries, 2004), 160.

39. C. S. Lewis, *The Weight of Glory* (1949; repr., HarperCollins, 2001), 30–31.